10-33

An Officer Down
Steps Back Up

D1113499

Laurie White

Suite 300 - 990 Fort St
Victoria, BC, V8V 3K2
Canada

www.friesenpress.com

ISBN
978-1-03-911574-3 (Hardcover)
78-1-03-911573-6 (Paperback)
978-1-03-911575-0 (eBook)

1. BIOGRAPHY & AUTOBIOGRAPHY, PERSONAL MEMOIRS

Distributed to the trade by The Ingram Book Company

Table of Contents

10-33: An Officer Down Steps Back Up is the memoir of an incredible young woman whose journey through traumatic injury provides insights and lessons we can all benefit from.

Laurie's story is full up heartbreaking, and yet uplifting. Although this book should be well read within the law enforcement profession, it should not be seen as a for-police-only volume. It is a story of the human experience in overcoming trauma and living with a disability.

This book is written from a deeply personal perspective, and that demands a lot of courage on the part of the author. Once I began to read "10-33", I found it difficult to put down.

Kevin M. Gilmartin, Ph.D.
Author of *Emotional Survival for Law Enforcement:*
A Guide for Officers and Their Families

Laurie White is, in one word, amazing! Reading her life story (so far) is to recognize one's own shortcomings because it is simply hard to imagine doing what she has done, despite being visited with severe trauma just as you are embarking on life and career. What a trooper and what an inspiration for others in policing and elsewhere. Mental and physical roadblocks are mere challenges to be overcome. That is what Laurie did, with grace, with determination, and with professionalism. She is the role model and, I can also attest, she is a lovely and warm human being who anyone would love to say, as I do, that she is their friend. Kudos, Laurie...

Peter M. German
Deputy Commissioner (ret'd)
RCMP

For my two favourite people - Rachel and Brett.
You are my reason for being.

And for my mom – Norah.
I couldn't have done any of this without you.

Foreword

In 1998, I was a member of the RCMP working in Saskatchewan. Cst. Laurie White was stationed at her first Detachment in Kitimat B.C. At 4:00pm on November 27th of that year, I went home from work. Laurie White did not. Instead, in the late afternoon of that day, she was rushed to the hospital, suffering from a devastating gunshot wound, and she almost died. It was a transformational moment, one that would negatively affect her life, forever … as an RCMP officer, as a wife and as a mother. This book describes that story and the lessons of her life until now, but it is clearly not the end of the story, nor does her near death shooting define the beginning of her journey. Laurie has chosen to tell, through an open-hearted first-person account, the chapters of her life, from her time as a young girl through her career in the Force, marked and transformed by her shooting, to the present day. This chronicle is both brutally frank and unflinchingly honest. She has unveiled some of her most secret dreams, and exposed her most unspeakable fears, and has combined them into a kind of "How to cope with crisis and tragedy 101" handbook. As you read through the chapters, you are allowed to know her very personal thoughts and observations, ones that show Laurie's vulnerabilities, but more importantly, her courage. Those of us who have not endured a moment that ultimately changes one's life forever, can only imagine and admire the determination, and feel the searing frustration, that it takes to get through every single day.

When I first met Laurie White in person, she was already back to work after her horrific injury, having managed the difficult hurdles of re-qualifying for police duties, both physically and psychologically. I was introduced to her with the description she so accurately stated: I was told that she was "the one who got shot". Contrary to her own sensitivities, that she had lost her self-esteem, and was feeling very frail, to me, she exuded confidence. I remember being so impressed and inspired by her spirit and determination. Her smile, and her personal presence, demanded a self-examination, about how much I had taken for granted in my career and my life.

But enough about me. This book is a challenge to everyone. It is a wake-up call to action; to make the most of one's life despite the challenges, and to be honest with oneself. I suspect this book has been cathartic for Laurie, but it has been a chronicle of strength for me. She has shown how a traumatic injury can crush not just your health, but your spirit as well. It also shows that the most brave of us, can survive and thrive to become a symbol of courage. Laurie joined the Force to be a positive influence and to help people … she is still doing that today with this amazing book.

Bev Busson, C.M., C.O.M., O.B.C.,

Commissioner, RCMP (retired)

Preface

This project is something I have long contemplated. Only now, after experiencing a lengthy period of upheaval—and ultimately, some enlightenment and a little bit of peace—have I found the catalyst to light a fire under my ass and complete this memoir.

Over the years, I have kept a junk box that corrals everything from media articles, inspirational books, and my own motivational speaking notes, to scraps of paper on which I have jotted down my thoughts and ideas. It is only now that I can say I have slowly, emotionally, and painstakingly waded through the items in this box and put some snippets of my life thus far to paper.

This is most certainly not meant to be a guidebook or a compilation of life lessons from a self-proclaimed self-help expert. These stories and opinions are mine. Memories of how things unfolded are my personal recollections; they are my own experiences and observations. My perceptions are simply my thoughts and are certainly not to be misconstrued to be anything but just that. They may not necessarily be everyone's memories, or everyone's truths, but they are my versions, and I own them. They are *my* legacy.

I faced a crash course in trauma and intensity near the outset of my career, and I was forced into an unexpected world. I learned, then, far more than I wanted to know, and I continue to learn now. The lessons I learned by no means sank in immediately. Time and distance shift one's perspective, and I know that my words and thoughts today are most certainly not what they would have been had I written this sooner.

I hope that when my children read this, they will understand their mom a little better—why after years of shared parenting, I may still cry when I trade them off for time with their dad; why I hug them often and squeeze them too tightly when I say goodbye; why I tell them and text them that I love them so frequently; why I feel personally offended for them when they are hurt or sad or upset; why I obsess about their safety. Hopefully, they will someday grasp the depth of my love for them.

The timing of this memoir is right for exactly right now. My journey has been both devastating and fulfilling, and I hope that in sharing my experiences with you, you will find some thread of commonality, something to which you can relate, and maybe even a few words from which you can glean something meaningful for your own life, wherever it finds you right now. This is a representation of me and is completely, unflinchingly honest, no matter how painful at times. I also hope that by sharing my deepest struggles and vulnerabilities and reflecting on my life and perspective, I, too, can continue to grow and heal and realize some newer and even more powerful life lessons.

As the famous NFL coach Vince Lombardi said, "It's not whether you get knocked down, it's whether you get up."

Part 1 –

Laying the
Foundation

Senses

Ears: POP! It sounded like a balloon popping. *Right* beside my head. My ears began to ring. They rang far more loudly than they did at the Rolling Stones concert I had attended in Toronto in 1989. I could barely hear over the buzzing, the ringing, the high-pitched roar.

Eyes: I saw a large, black, gaping hole in the bright, white townhouse door in front of me. Smoke was coming from that hole.

Nose: I smelled the distinctly familiar smell of gunpowder. My nostrils were attacked, instantly covered in a layer of dust. I was overcome by the offensive odour.

Taste: My mouth, though it was closed, could taste the gritty residue.

Touch: I felt a shock—a burning, searing, red-hot, flaming sensation in my right shin. It was a pain like no other. None. My leg was on fire.

Bewildered, I looked down and saw grey-ish, white-ish, black-ish smoke billowing from my right shin.

It was bizarre, so surreal to have every one of my senses kick in, to be so acutely aware of my surroundings, and my body, yet still be utterly confused about what had just happened.

Then it dawned on me.

Standing there, still unable to grasp the reality, the gravity, I said to my partner, "I've been shot."

He looked at me, eyes wide, and said in disbelief, "What?"

"I've been shot," I repeated.

The colour drained from his face. "Well, lie down!" he commanded.

Obediently but gingerly, I lay down on my left side, carefully manoeuvring my injured right leg on top of my left leg for support. My heart was thumping out of my chest and straight into my throat. Horrific pain was coursing through my body. Everything was buzzing—my ears, my body, my heart.

And then I heard my partner use the portable radio code every police officer dreads.

"10-33."

It meant, "Officer down."

It meant there was a major emergency. It meant send help *immediately.*

And *I* was that "officer down."

"Normal Life"

It all began in 1993. Unable to find a job after graduate school, I was busily running around my hometown of Brockville, Ontario, juggling substitute teaching, bartending, coaching skating, and instructing aerobics. It was a hectic schedule, one that required that I be flexible and willing to jump into action at a moment's notice, demanding lots of eating in the car and frequent clothing changes. That life was a far cry from the one I had envisioned for myself when I had graduated university—twice. Nope, throughout my high school and university years, I had never once looked towards my future and pictured myself at twenty-three years old, with a master's degree, living back home with my parents, slinging drinks at the local roadhouse!

My self-esteem was taking a serious beating on a daily basis, and the progressively increasing negativity was resulting in a rapidly growing chip on my shoulder. Every morning I would jump if the family home phone rang between 6 and 7 a.m. Most days I actually wanted it to ring, even though I often hadn't gotten home from bartending until well after midnight. I would groggily answer "definitely" to the high school secretary asking if I could come in and substitute-teach that day. I would pull on my teaching clothes and race to the school for opening bell. I was a physical education grad, so if I were lucky, I would be assigned a day of gym classes. I would get to play dodgeball, spot gymnastics tricks, or join in a volleyball scrimmage. If I were not so lucky, I would sit in history or French class, sometimes with no lesson plan left by the regular teacher. I would corral kids into the classroom, close the door, and try my best to keep them relatively quiet while we entertained each other for seventy-five very long minutes. And I was paid well for all of it.

After school I laced up my skates and stood bundled up on the community ice surface in Athens, Ontario, teaching skating lessons to young children. The lessons for three-year-olds involved a lot of teaching those timeless classics: the Hokey Pokey and the Bird Dance. The older skaters learned mohawks, three-turns, bunny-hops, and waltz jumps. We enthusiastically choreographed thirty-second solos to tunes like the Pink Panther theme song, transferred carefully onto cassettes from the portable CD player I proudly carried with me. I recall the joy that went into presenting my students with their very own solo music cassette tape; I painstakingly created those musical masterpieces at home while shushing my parents and brothers. Any background noise my family created during production was exaggerated and magnified on the arena's sound system.

During the evenings I would put on a mini-skirt and serve draft beer and chicken wings to the local, mostly men's hockey and ball teams. I also regularly waited on my various local family members and friends. I would serve up our specialty Jukebox Long Island Iced Teas and Cocaines (a lethal combination of Bailey's, amaretto, vodka, Kahlua, shaken with milk on ice and topped with a splash of Diet Coke) in hopes that I over-measured (read: free pour) just enough to allow for a leftover sip or two for myself. I made popcorn in the industrial-sized machine and consumed an alarming amount of it for dinner many nights a week. The bar's sound system played Brooks & Dunn's "Neon Moon" and "Lost & Found" on repeat. I still know every word to both.

Interspersed throughout my week were many step aerobics classes. I wore the obligatory body suits with high-cut bottoms. I wore neon-coloured leggings or tight bike shorts paired with a crop top, but my courage to expose my mid-section would usually fade last minute and I would throw on a loose muscle shirt over top. I peppered my classes with motivational phrases and shouted, "Eight more, seven, six, now five …" countless times. I thoroughly enjoyed leading the participants through a sweaty hour of

Salt-n-Pepa ("Push It") and C+C Music Factory ("Gonna Make You Sweat (Everybody Dance Now)").

But although I was keeping busy and trying desperately to pay off my student loans from university, I was absolutely not moving in the direction I had envisioned.

Despite my best efforts in searching for suitable, longer-term, meaningful, rewarding, consistent, and engaging employment with a steady and sustainable paycheque, I was having zero luck. I was submitting job applications often. Very often. And I was submitting them everywhere, all over Ontario. I scoured newspapers for help-wanted advertisements, and I entertained ideas about working in all kinds of fields, some of which I had never even known existed until stumbling upon an ad.

Pharmaceutical sales? Sure. I could learn the medical lingo and would be interested in travelling for work.

Teaching? I had changed my mind after third-year university and had chosen to do a master's degree instead. That ship had sailed.

Marketing? Maybe I could capitalize on my interpersonal skills.

Physiotherapy? That would require a third university degree, and I would need more money, and therefore more student loans, to do that. Hmmm …

Would I move? Yes!

Would I care if I made a crummy starting salary? No!

I just wanted to start being a reasonably well-intentioned post-university grown-up and live the lifestyle I felt I had earned. And deserved. I wanted to move forward. And out of my parents' house!

Every day, I would race down the lengthy driveway to the roadside mailbox at my parents' rural address, only to open yet another what I called PFO letter––a "please fuck off" letter––telling me I was too this, not enough that, needed more something. Every letter weighed heavily on me and made me feel increasingly demoralized, useless, frustrated. I felt as if each letter brought criticism and judgment. No matter how I looked at it, I wasn't enough. My hopes were slowly dissolving, so for months I continued to bartend in my mini-skirts, teach skating in my turtlenecks, instruct aerobics in my high-cut bodysuits, teach school in my carefully pressed business casual attire. Outwardly, I put on a good show; inwardly, my self-esteem was plummeting, and my confidence was rapidly disappearing.

Detours and Rerouting

In my youth, I believed life was all about choices. I learned that it was important to set attainable goals and strategize about how to reach those goals. As I matured and learned more complex lessons about right from wrong, I became further convinced of what constituted my moral compass. That, in turn, allowed me to become more and more confident that my principle-driven, ethical goal-setting would never fail me. I could rely on myself, and I believed that consistently and successfully choosing the "right" turns would ultimately result in my overall "success" in life. I looked at it as if life were a series of daily choices, choices that *must* be made correctly. Each choice was mine to make, and the more often I made the right choices, the smoother my path and the better my life would be. For so long, it seemed simple and straightforward. And then it wasn't. Because, despite making solid decisions, like I thought I was doing in my twenties, I realized that things can and do get derailed. Detours are unavoidable.

While I still believe that planning is a critical life skill, my conclusion now is that, despite any amount of planning, life is also an amazingly complex series of happenings. Those chance happenings are frequent, often profound, and completely and utterly out of our control. They occur in spite of any decisions we make.

Ceasing to continually fight to gain and retain that elusive power over how things turn out has allowed me to surrender myself to better accept the inevitable detours, to find peace amidst the constant rerouting. I'm grateful that, as evidenced by some of the turns my life has taken, even best-laid plans when not realized, can bring a great deal of joy, personal satisfaction, and enlightenment.

3 Percent Short at Wallyworld

I am the only daughter and the third of four children. I grew up with my brothers (Dave, Rob, and Steve) as well as both parents (Norah and Wally) in Wallyworld ... in Brockville, Ontario. Wallyworld (named after our dad) is the affectionate name we called our family home. My childhood was good, easy, busy, and fun, and gatherings there are the source of many fond memories held by our family and many friends.

Mom is originally from a northern Ontario mining town. She had graduated from university in Toronto and had moved back to be a teacher there when my dad, a farmer, showed up in town as a new elementary school teacher and football coach. They were married quickly and then settled in Brockville, Ontario. My brothers and I learned early on about the importance of hard work as my mom supported my dad while he became a secondary school teacher. He earned both his bachelor's degree and his master's degree while working full-time, all while navigating their first chaotic years of marriage, together with a rapidly growing brood of children.

In high school in the '80s, I returned home one day after skating, a sport I did almost every single day from September until June. My father, sitting in his usual spot at the head of the dining room table, looked up at me and asked how my science test at school that day had gone. Arrogantly, I announced, "97 percent!" Without missing a beat, my father said, "What happened to the other 3 percent?"

Now some people would view this exchange as being a negative one. Some would think my dad was being exceptionally hard on me. Others, who knew me and who knew my dad, would not. In fact, those people would understand.

The reality was that, in that academic unit, I was capable of achieving 100 percent, and my dad was well aware of this. However, at that time in my life I was mostly focused on my social life and skating. But mostly my social life. As a guidance counsellor at my high school, Dad knew exactly what my priorities were. I liked school well enough, and my grades were decent. Despite that 97 percent test result, I was no Ontario Scholar (like my eldest brother). I was not going to be receiving a full-ride academic/athletic scholarship to an Ivy League university (like my second-oldest brother). But my dad was reminding me that he knew that if I had applied myself, and spent some time studying instead of socializing, I *could* have achieved 100 percent.

In that moment when my dad challenged me about the 3 percent, I was indignant and defensive; after all, 97 percent is an excellent result! But over time, I realized that his comment was in fact a valuable lesson, a lesson about much more than a science test. Giving subpar effort is apparent to other people, and my dad had called me on it. In that situation, it wasn't about praise for 97 percent; rather, it was intended to be a reality check about being capable of more.

Doing well is commendable, sure. But I realized that doing well while knowing I could be better, do better, is simply settling. Settling is being complacent and lazy. It is accepting being comfortable, accepting less of myself. Dad was reminding me that it was time to apply myself, to consider my potential. He was encouraging me to want to feel true pride because true pride comes from hard work. I could take pride in any result, 97 percent or not, as long as I had actually put forth some effort and *tried*.

True character, and striving for that extra little bit, counts.

3 percent matters.

Asking and Assuming

At one point when I was a child, we lived across the street from a family who had a pool. We, on the other hand, had no pool, nor did we have air conditioning, so on hot, humid summer days, I would put on my bathing suit and casually sit on my front step, hoping for an invitation to go for a dip at the neighbours' house. The neighbours had twin boys who were friends of my younger brother, and the boys had little interest in hanging out with me unless I could occasionally suit up and stand in as goalie for a raucous game of road hockey. I would wait and wait on the step in my bathing suit, looking forlorn and sweaty and uncomfortable, trying to draw attention to my plight. Sometimes, a pity invitation to that pool materialized; more often, it didn't.

Too frequently, we find ourselves waiting in different ways––maybe not for an invitation to cool off in a neighbour's pool, but for that next ping notification, for that next rush of adrenaline that comes from our devices. We wait to be offered a new position at work, to be noticed or acknowledged. We wait for things to happen *to* us, rather than making them happen for ourselves. We rely on others instead of ourselves.

When I was in high school and attending my second of what would end up being three proms, we were instructed to make our menu choices several weeks in advance. Options were either chicken or filet mignon.

Naïve in many ways and far from a foodie (my dining experiences on dates thus far had consisted mostly of Swiss Chalet), I felt my only option was chicken. Why? Because the only other option was fish. I assumed that since "filet mignon" starts with "filet," it was fish. I disliked fish; therefore, I chose chicken for the prom dinner. By the same logic, so did my friend. Simple.

Prom night arrived and I was happily socializing when my friend and I were presented with very nice-looking pieces of chicken. Others at our table, however, were presented with their much more appealing and delectable pieces of steak. "Steak!" I thought indignantly. "How did *they* get steak?" my friend and I asked each other.

When we commented at our table about the unfairness of our dining partners receiving steak, we were reminded of the pre-selection menu. We were told that they had selected the filet mignon. Embarrassed, I realized my mistake, and they all laughed when my friend and I admitted we thought filet mignon was fish, not steak.

What I learned was that instead of making an assumption and acknowledging *I didn't actually know* what filet mignon was, I simply could have asked for clarification. Had I just inquired about the menu when we initially had a choice, I too could have enjoyed delicious steak instead of salivating over everyone else's!

Contrary to what I used to believe, asking for what I want, instead of hoping someone else is a mind-reader and should simply know, is critical. I no longer want to wait, hoping someone recognizes that I want to cool off with a swim.

I also recognize that saying, "I don't know" and asking questions for clarification does not represent weakness. Or a lack of intelligence. Not having an answer for every single thing does not shake my confidence or reduce my credibility. I have learned that, in fact, quite the opposite is true. Admitting I don't know is humanizing. And relatable. And rapport-building. When I don't know an answer, I want to remain open to finding one.

I want to stop assuming, and I want to be unafraid to ask questions, because I love to swim, and I don't want to settle for chicken when I truly want steak.

New Directions

By 1995, after two years of my chaotic, unfulfilling post-university life, I no longer wanted to spend my time waiting. I wanted to take back little bits of myself. I wanted to create opportunities for myself, to make things happen instead of relinquishing that power to others.

While at the gym one day, I happened to meet a local Royal Canadian Mounted Police (RCMP) officer. The RCMP is the Canadian federal police force. Where I grew up, there is a smaller municipal police force for policing within city limits. For many years, we lived just out of that city, so our house fell under the provincial police force's jurisdiction. My city, however, was on a U.S. border, and there were a few RCMP members around our area. The member I met spoke highly of the RCMP as a career and encouraged me to apply. I had never seriously considered policing, but the work, he said, was people-oriented and all about helping others. It was unpredictable and interesting, and opportunities with our federal police force were vast. I could be posted anywhere in the country, and the organization was so large that moving around happened regularly. Even more appealing to me was the fact that policing is an indisputably respectable profession. After all, I was outgoing and physically fit, and the RCMP would most certainly offer the employment stability I desperately craved.

Intrigued by this new possibility, I began the application process. I was open to anything and everything! I completed numerous background check forms, submitted university transcripts and copies of my degrees. I conscientiously looked up addresses of the various places I had lived while in university, sourced out contact information for several bosses and character references--no simple feat in the pre-internet era of 1995. I continued working my four jobs and frequently rollerbladed in my spare time with our beloved family dog, King, who had become my fitness training partner.

Months later I was working a day shift at the bar when a man came in alone and ordered lunch. I didn't know him, and because we had so many regular customers, I knew he was from out of town. He was busy doing paperwork and didn't talk much, so naturally I assumed he was a travelling businessman. When he seemed to be close to finishing, he asked me if my name was Laurie White. Eyebrows raised, I nodded. Why did this stranger know my name? He introduced himself as an RCMP member who had come specifically to observe me. He was there to watch me in my workplace, to see how I presented myself, how I interacted with customers and staff. He was doing background checks on me, and the paperwork he had busied himself with at the barstool was all about me!

My mind was racing, worriedly reviewing and analyzing everything that had transpired since he had arrived and placed his order. I kept wondering if I had been rude to anyone, botched an order, or generally just let the large chip on my shoulder show to anyone in my vicinity. *Sigh* ...

The RCMP application process consists of many steps, and it was a very time-consuming and stressful phase, so when I received that call to visit Kingston, Ontario, for my applicant interview, I was understandably nervous. I carefully chose my interview-appropriate outfit and drove the hour to the Kingston Detachment, trying not to wrinkle my clothes. What ensued was a gruelling four-hour interview. The member interviewing me asked all the basic, predictable questions about my education, my work experience, and my motivation for applying to the RCMP. Next, he began asking me to tell him about friends of mine who were of different cultural backgrounds.

"Tell me about your friends with different beliefs."

"Well, I'm Catholic and I went to Catholic school, so most of my friends are also Catholic. There are a few who are Protestant and Anglican, but mostly if my friends go to church, they are Catholic."

"Tell me about your friends with different heritages, different cultural backgrounds."

"Um ... "

The interviewer was Black, and I most certainly didn't know how to appropriately phrase my responses. My life, up until that point, had been very "non-diverse." It wasn't that I intentionally avoided such interpersonal situations or relationships; it was simply that opportunities hadn't existed. Brockville was simply not a diverse place then. I didn't have any close friends of other ethnicities who spoke other languages, practised other religions, had different skin colours. I remember very few details of that interview, but I do remember well how awkwardly I handled that line of questioning and how uncomfortable it was searching for acceptable ways of expressing myself honestly to a person with a different background. I remember how worried I was that my lack of exposure to other groups of people would end up being perceived negatively and ultimately prevent me from being accepted into the RCMP.

Months later, my naivete was sorely reinforced. I had successfully progressed through the application phase and arrived at "Depot", the iconic RCMP training academy in Regina, Saskatchewan. I excitedly moved into my dorm room and began the process of getting to know the other five women in my troop. I was chatting with my first-ever Indo-Canadian friend when I noticed that her one allotted photo on her desk was of an older man with a beard. Most people at Depot reserved that coveted photo space for a spouse, a partner, or children. Naturally, I asked her if the man in the photo was her father. With a mixture of disbelief and amusement, she patiently explained to me that that was her religious leader. The only religious leader I would have recognized was Jesus, and her photo was not of him.

In the decades that have passed since that time, my exposure to different cultures, races, and backgrounds has increased immensely, and my life experiences have been enhanced as a result. I have learned how some cultures grieve and how some celebrate. I have witnessed some interesting traditions and participated in some powerful ceremonies.

Floundering in a job interview can undoubtedly be embarrassing. Being asked questions about sensitive topics and being uncomfortable with how to respond feels risky and extremely awkward. But I also recognize and appreciate that my feelings during those experiences stemmed from a legitimate place of innocence, openness, and a genuine willingness to learn. Since I never want to stop learning, I must accept those risks and continue to expand my horizons.

Depot

At Depot, the training academy for every RCMP officer, I became a "cadet" and would join five women and eighteen men in making up Troop 12, 1995-1996.

The day I arrived at Depot, I was struggling with my ridiculously oversized trunk, attempting to steer it through the entrance door of my new dormitory building. Sweating profusely and cursing myself under my breath for always succumbing to the need to over-pack, I was fortunate to look up into a pair of friendly, warm, sympathetic, brown eyes. Lorelei was her name, and she graciously offered to assist me in carrying my cumbersome trunk up the flights of stairs to my floor. My dorm, as it turned out, was also hers. When we finally reached our assigned space, I flung open the door and looked around in wide-eyed dismay. While I had lived in a university dorm before, this was no university dorm. This was one long, narrow bedroom, more like an extra-wide hallway, with sixteen beds on either side. There were tiny desks and closets symmetrically placed along each side. As a girl with only brothers, and having never shared a bedroom, I realized I was now expected to share my new bedroom for the next six-plus months with—gulp—thirty-one other women!

With Lorelei.

Lorelei, also the only girl out of four siblings, and I became "pit partners" due to the alphabetical order of our last name. During our time at Depot, we forged an unbreakable bond: she has been my most cherished friend and trusted confidante since 1995. Lor is kind-hearted, warm, intelligent, charming, articulate, and very, very funny. I am forever grateful for her support.

Lor and I shared our tiny, designated space—a small "pit" consisting of two cots with thin, lumpy mattresses; two small dressers; and two tiny closets. The beds, we quickly learned, were to be made only with RCMP-issued and -approved bedding— thin, stiff sheets; flat pillows; and prickly wool blankets. They were to be made mili-tary-style, with sheets ironed and blankets folded in a specific manner. Each bed had to be made to certain standards, and they all had to look the same, the same as our pit partner's and the same as the other thirty-one cadet's beds. Our soon-to-be

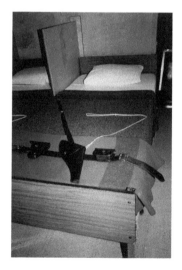

Depot dormitory bed.

highly polished Sam Browne belt and holster, to be worn with our coveted red serge, were to be displayed ceremoniously across the always-made bed.

Our closets were to be organized in a pre-determined, uniform manner, with clothing hangers displaying only specific items of clothing, spaced in a certain way. Drawers were organized in a similar way.

There was a small cupboard above each closet, a closet barely big enough to be of use. (Funnily enough, a few brave and nimble cadets of smaller stature went so far as to sleep in that cupboard on nights before a drill inspection!)

The floors were expected to shine. Always. No scuffs. As if they had just been varnished with a coat of clear nail polish.

On our desktops, we were permitted to display only pre-determined items, including a single framed photo of our loved ones.

Each pit, eight per side, was to be meticulously maintained by the pair of cadets living in it. My side of the pit mirrored Lorelei's. Each of our beds was then separated from neighbouring pits by a small snoreboard, a thin, short wooden board propped upright between cots to prevent one cadet from breathing directly on his or her neighbour. The snoreboard served only as a partial blockage, however, as it ran only half the length of a cot and did nothing to keep knees and feet from interfering with snoreboard partners at night.

Any oversight or lack of attention to detail could, and sometimes did, result in our pits being "tossed" (deliberately ransacked) by unhappy drill instructors. It could also result in punishment for our entire troop, so no one wanted any blame placed on him or her. We were encouraged to work together as a team to ensure we all succeeded because any individual failure could result in group repercussions.

Like thousands of Depot predecessors, I would spend six-plus months learning self-defence, boxing, ground-fighting techniques, and martial arts.

I would learn about enforcing laws and the Canadian Criminal Code, as well as various provincial statutes.

I would learn proper arrest procedures and search techniques.

I would learn radio terminology and police 10-codes.

I would spend countless hours learning and practising effective use-of-force options, including police batons and pepper spray. I would personally be exposed to pepper spray and tear gas to teach me how to function under the influence of those substances, should the situation ever arise out in the field.

I would learn police driving skills and feel the adrenaline rush of learning to drive, in a controlled fashion, at high speeds through an obstacle course.

I would hold firearms for the first time in my life. I would learn pistol, rifle, and shotgun tactics and safe storage. I would polish my service-issue revolver until it sparkled. I would learn how it worked and how to care for it. I would learn to treat it like a precious piece of shiny jewellery. Later, I would pride myself on becoming an excellent target shooter.

I would obsess about physical fitness, running, and lifting weights. I would run miles, hating every step. Although I was fit, make no mistake about it, I had *never* been a runner. The unwelcome exertion on my non-runner's physique resulted in a serious stress fracture in my ankle, one which, for a time, seriously threatened my graduation from Depot. I would do countless push-ups and sit-ups. I would learn to climb ropes. I would stress about my body weight; if cadets were found to be above whatever mysteriously established weight that had been assigned to him or her, it meant that that cadet had to attend daily "Piggy Parade." Piggy Parade consisted of standing at attention in the drill hall with other weight "offenders," staring at oneself in the mirror and chanting, "I am a piggy." They were efforts to shame cadets into losing the weight, according to someone else's baseless observation about what was supposedly acceptable for that individual.

I would stress about passing the Physical Abilities Requirement Evaluation, the P.A.R.E. The P.A.R.E. test is the timed physical standard mandatory test required for all RCMP officers to graduate from Depot training. It is a simulated foot chase and physical struggle, designed as an obstacle course. This test is timed, consisting of six laps in a figure-eight shape. The laps include jumps, stairs, and lying down and getting up, and at the end of the test there is a push and pull weight station. It concludes with a heavy bag carry. The whole test is designed to simulate a police situation involving chasing, controlling, and apprehending a suspect. To be accepted into the RCMP, we were required to perform the P.A.R.E. in four-and-a-half minutes, but to graduate from training we had to complete it in under four minutes.

We would spend hours learning drill manoeuvres. At the outset of training, we were issued ugly brown pants and were required to wear our sneakers. As the most junior cadets, any time we moved around base, we had to move in double-time (a light jog), with our fists pressed to our chests. We had to jog on the roadways and were not permitted to use sidewalks.

Every stage in training was a privilege earned. We would take great pride in being able to progress from wearing ugly brown pants to our issued "blues," our navy pants with the yellow stripes. We were thrilled when we earned the right to march on the campus sidewalks, not jog on the roadways like the newbies. Blues and sidewalk rights are earned via a well-established process, and these privileges are highly coveted symbols of experience. How and where we moved, as well as what we wore, indicated seniority on base. We only earned those rights when, as a troop, we demonstrated, in a variety of ways, that we were responsible, knowledgeable, cohesive, and able to function as a team. We only received them when we showed we deserved them, and as we navigated the training program, we were increasingly filled with pride.

We would iron our clothes obsessively, concerned about the precise crease location from RCMP shoulder flash to the end of the sleeve. We would study each of our troopmates with an analytical eye to ensure we were all conforming and impeccable. We knew that something as simple as a forgotten name tag could result in the entire troop being punished.

One day during a drill class in December, and against the advice of our Right Marker (our troop leader), I opted to forego my drill cap in exchange for a furry, red Santa hat. Given the festive season, I felt it was worth an attempt at gauging the sense of humour our ever-so-strict drill corporal may or may not have had. No one else felt it necessary to test him, but I needed to amuse myself. We went to drill class and stood obediently at attention, presenting our shiny, well-groomed selves for initial inspection.

The corporal slowly made his way up and down our two rows, in front and in back, inspecting each of us from head to toe. He made observations, some funny, some not, criticizing many of us. As he approached me, I wondered why I had thought wearing a Santa hat was at all even remotely amusing. I was grinning stupidly, slightly nervously, fully expecting to be lambasted loudly and ordered to do several sets of push-ups for attempting such a silly shenanigan. Instead, he stopped, looked me in the eyes and shook his head slowly like I was a misbehaving toddler. But at least he smiled. I did have to do several push-ups as punishment, but I know he was mildly entertained. It was a minor risk, a goofy move for sure, but one that to me symbolized my need for finding some short-lived respite from the daily grind, the conformity, and the lack of sleep.

I would spend six months being referred to by my surname, "White." I would wear that name in block letters on plain white T-shirts, print it with Sharpie on my Hanes underwear so it wouldn't get mixed up with Lorelei's Hanes underwear in our joint coin-laundry adventures. I still have "WHITE" labelled on pant hangers that used to proudly display my RCMP-issued blues in our tiny Depot closet.

I seldom slept. I would lie awake worrying about reaching predetermined standards in every single area of training, physical and otherwise. Not reaching those targets meant failure, failure that meant we would be immediately kicked out, sent home, and would not graduate with our troopmates. We had already lost two troop members and I most certainly did not want that number to increase.

I would learn to eat meals in seconds flat to get to our next academic class or activity. Sustenance was necessary but more of an inconvenience, and I can still pound food in record time!

I would painstakingly polish boots and research tricks to speed up the polishing process while still achieving optimal results. No one wanted to have dull, scuffed boots; after all, we were privileged to be able to wear them, but we also had studying, ironing, physical training, and floors to buff!

I would spend hours meticulously pressing and arranging bedsheets and issued uniform items. Initially, the expectations seemed so silly, but over time, they led me to understand that such menial tasks taught us about teamwork and paying close attention to detail, both critical skills for effective police officers. With formal inspections looming periodically and at unpredictable intervals, I would worry about being the one troop member whose minor oversight led to all our dorms being tossed or worse, "CB'd." CB'd meant "confined to barracks." Certain privileges would be denied; essentially, we were grounded!

Lorelei and I would team up for chores; I would iron our clothing while she buffed our floor. I happily relinquished buffing duties after several unsuccessful attempts. Despite my good intentions, the uncooperative beast of a machine would suddenly lurch out of control and upend our well-made beds! Sometimes I would do my ironing and polishing and tidying while consuming forbidden rum (squirreled away in that aforementioned giant trunk in the storage room) mixed with Diet Coke (from the pop machine in the basement) and snacking on stinky, but yummy, corn nuts.

I would book into hotel rooms in the city on weekends, just for respite, to get away from the pressure. I would put on my cowboy boots, tease my wavy hair, then hairspray it so it stayed big, and I would learn two-stepping at the local country bar.

I would wear little to no makeup. I would learn all kinds of nifty up-do hair tricks because long hair had to be styled in a non-hazardous manner. Many female cadets would be so exasperated by the ongoing hair hassle that they would give up and cut their hair off. Some would go entirely with a cropped cut. Others would shave the section of hair that fell below their forage cap in the back and leave the top/front part longer. This way it could be tucked into the hat when needed and fall down and cover the almost-bald part in the evenings and on weekends. Me, I couldn't fathom either of those choices, so I spent a lot of money on extra-hold hair gel, hair spray, and a ridiculously large collection of hair clips. I became a master French-braider so that I could tuck my hair into my uniform hats during the day but let it go loose and flowy at night. It was my feeble attempt to maintain some sense of femininity, some individuality, during a very what-seemed-to-be masculinizing time in my life.

We would become so excited during scenarios, simulated calls for police staged by paid actors. The uncertainty of what we could possibly face out on the road was an absolute rush! We play-acted and rehearsed our soon-to-be real-life responsibilities in a controlled environment, learning strategies and putting our new skills to the test. It gave us a taste for the unpredictable kinds of policing duties and challenges we would encounter out in the field in the communities where we would be assigned.

The theme of my life had become "conforming." We squeezed into too-tight forage caps—hats determined only to fit properly when a fist pounding down on it from above made your forehead skin squish down towards your eyeballs. This type of snug fit also ensured that the hat would stay in place when punishment push-ups were doled out, and often resulted in one helluva headache. Pants were made with uncomfortable, scratchy, unforgiving wool. Waistbands of the women's style of pants sat uncomfortably above our actual waists. We wore clip-on ties that dug into our necks, which were already constricted by the tight buttoned-up fit of our uniform shirts. Neckbands of our red serge uniforms had stiff Velcro, which, when done up properly, made us feel like our airways were compromised. We squeezed our bodies into heavy gunbelts for hours and hours on end. We developed strategies to slide in and out of police car seats without getting stuck on the steering wheel or the seatbelt strap while also being careful not to dislodge any of our equipment. We gradually grew accustomed to our new normal, our new routines, our new uniforms, our new images. We worked as a team, as a troop. We were unified and cohesive—mostly—progressively moulding nicely into exactly what was expected of an increasingly senior cadet and soon-to-be Mountie.

I would spend the duration of training exhausted, pre-occupied only with my successful completion of the arduous training program of our iconic national police force. I had wholeheartedly thrown myself into my new world. Although I hadn't been one of the cadets who had known their whole life that they wanted to become a police officer, I sure knew it now.

Comfort Zones

During police training at Depot, there was a swimming requirement as part of our physical training. I was a decent swimmer, but my stroke techniques were by no means those of an accomplished swimmer. I blame that on the fact that as a child taking lessons, I had been told I had to do mouth-to-mouth resuscitation on a boy I hated! This was long before the days of having dummy dolls to practise such lifesaving skills. It was a time of awkward pre-adolescence, and the boy's lips were big and perpetually moist—from his tongue and teeth and mouth, *not* the pool water. I was going to fail that childhood swimming course if I didn't effectively demonstrate just how well I could seal his big, wet lips with my own and perform artificial respiration. So there I was, kneeling down, my freckled face hovering over his yucky mouth, avoiding direct eye contact, with the swimming instructor waiting impatiently for me to get past the grossness. My heart was beating fast, and my mind was racing. I took a big breath, closed my eyes, leaned in closer, bringing my face ever so slightly nearer his. And I panicked. I just couldn't do it. I quit swimming lessons that day.

So, when I was in Depot so many years later, we were issued—gulp—Speedos. Yes, Speedos! There were no carefully chosen, figure-flattering options. There were no tummy-slimming, waist-enhancing, butt-flattering, bust-enlarging SwimCo suits. Females were issued the shapeless, one-piece, saggy-boob-enhancing, navy, almost transparent women's versions.

Males were issued the standard, tight, small, revealing (very revealing), navy Olympic brief-style versions.

We would march to the pool building in uniform and anxiously await dismissal from our troop formation. That would signal us to hurry to the change room. It would be a mad dash with clothes flying all around us as we rushed to don our much-loathed RCMP-issued suits. The objective, we had quickly learned, was to change as fast as possible so that you could rapidly enter the pool area and submerge your body into the water. It was a race; a hasty transition meant there were fewer witnesses! Speed could somewhat hide the bathing suits and very slightly minimize feelings of humiliation. Troopmates who were slower to change would self-consciously exit the change room with hands strategically placed in a futile attempt to cover their private parts. They would be subjected to giggling and ridicule from those who had submerged more rapidly.

On the first day of swimming, we realized that two of our troopmates did not know how to swim. RCMP swimming requirements were not stringent, but there were requirements, nonetheless. As my two troopmates stood there, trembling in fear, on the sidelines of the pool, being yelled at by our instructors to jump in, I was in disbelief. They were scared, and rightly so. I cannot imagine standing there, in front of peers, feeling terrified, self-conscious, and pressured to do something so frightening. The rest of us felt compassion and empathy, not fully understanding the depth of what they were being asked to do. Collectively, we encouraged them. After a few moments, and a great deal of support, they both jumped into the deep water. We cheered loudly when they surfaced, sputtering and flailing, laughing nervously. We helped them to the sides of the pool, feeling so much admiration for what they had just done. It was powerful to witness. That day, we all learned a valuable lesson about stepping outside our comfort zones, supporting our colleagues, respecting them while they took their own time to grapple with their individual anxieties. We were inspired witnessing them prove themselves. We felt good about encouraging them to take risks, and their confidence took an almost palpable boost.

Many years later, I was newly dating a person who loved to ski. I, on the other hand, have never been a skier and had only been an amputee for just over a year. I was scared. I was nervous. How could I ski? What equipment would I need? Where would I find the confidence to try such a sport? But he wanted to ski, I wanted to please him, and despite my trepidation, I was eager to take on a new challenge. We went to the rental kiosk, and after many adjustments to my prosthetic leg in my ski boot, I was ready. Equipment was heavy and cumbersome, and I was awkward and slow, but I made my way to the lift and was transported up the mountain. I stood at the top of the bunny hill, terrified, and I looked down watching four-year-olds fearlessly race down the hill. Speeds seemed too fast, and I felt much too incapable of attempting this unfamiliar sport. My boyfriend reminded me of the tips he had shared with me the day before. He reminded me of body positions, of foot placement, and how to position my poles. I looked up at him, looked back at the ski run in front of me, took a breath, and I skied. Not well, but I skied. I was scared out of my wits, and it wasn't physically easy. That day, I fell and laughed and fell and laughed some more. But I did it. And it was actually fun, exhilarating even! In doing something that initially began with me feeling like I was doing something for someone else, I ended up stepping outside my comfort zone and doing something for myself.

I retired from skiing that day but that, along with my fellow cadets' first swimming experience, taught me that fear can be overcome with solid preparation, a little moral support, some humility, and a lot of laughter!

Graduation!

On March 11, 1996, my graduation day from Depot, I was brimming with pride. I was happy and healthy, beaming with excitement. I was nervous about embarking on my next adventure, but I was so ready. It was a future that no one I had known before my arrival at Depot had ever experienced.

Our troop's loved ones flew in from all over the country to witness our graduation ceremony. We put on demonstrations of our newly acquired law enforcement training skills. We showed off our athletic prowess and our accomplishments in every area.

Our "pass-out" drill performance in front of family and friends was exceptional. It was moving and powerful and highlighted the culmination of six months of superior training and teamwork.

Afterwards, we consumed much rum and celebrated by dancing to the "Macarena."

And so, my coveted, dreamed-of, true "post-university, adult life," finally free from the dreaded PFO letters, began. I had achieved what, just six months prior, I had not even known I had so desperately wanted. I was now a member of the prestigious RCMP!

A very excited Constable White with Constable Wirachowsky (in 1996)!

Where the Hell is Kitimat?

In the final weary weeks of training at Depot, we anxiously awaited our postings. When I had departed for training in August 1995, I had been told that there was a good chance of being posted back to Ontario upon graduation the following March, but I learned quickly after arriving at Depot that that was unlikely. When I had been requested by human resources to identify my top three provinces, I ignored all the rumours about where I would likely be sent and completed my wish-list forms. I chose:

1. Ontario

2. Alberta

3. B.C.

Weeks later, I learned that I was assigned to B.C., my third choice. At that time, and like everyone in my troop, the specific location within each of our designated provinces remained a secret, and therefore the source of all kinds of what-ifs and conjecture.

All the uncertainty was exhausting, and naturally we were very preoccupied with our upcoming postings. As with most things at Depot, when it was time to receive that information, assignments were announced alphabetically. As each troopmate's surname before "W" was being called, my head was spinning. I could hardly focus. Where would I be going? What would it be like? How far from home would it be?

And finally, "White ... Kitimat!"

"Where the *hell* is Kitimat?" I asked myself, mind racing.

With each member of Troop 12's postings now identified and publicly shared, I anxiously awaited our troop's dismissal so I could reference a map. When I found one, I began searching the area around Vancouver. Since Vancouver is the largest city in B.C., that made sense as a starting point and frankly, if you're not from B.C., it seems like Vancouver *is* B.C.!

But I couldn't find Kitimat; it wasn't near Vancouver. Much to my dismay, my forefinger leading the frantic paper map search found its way via concentric circles around Vancouver, north … north … more north! Kitimat was definitely not close to Vancouver! Not at all.

But now that our first postings were identified, excitement grew rapidly, and time flew by at Depot. Days were a blur, and I was given only a few days to fly home and wrap up my former life as I knew it. I spent a chaotic few days shopping for furniture so the movers could load my belongings on a truck and transport them far, far away. It seemed surreal as I said an emotional and very tearful goodbye to my family and found myself about to board a plane departing the Ottawa airport. I had carefully followed all the RCMP-issued uniform packing instructions, and my belongings were arranged in my baggage according to the directions I had been provided. Nervously, I made my way to the ticket counter to check my baggage. Blurry-eyed from my tears, I picked up my boarding pass and proceeded to the security gate, waving and trying to smile for my parents, hoping I looked convincingly excited instead of terrified. There, I was greeted by an airline staff member who coldly informed me that transporting my police-issued kit—specifically, my police baton—in my carry-on bag was not allowed. As he stated, doing so was contrary to airport security protocols. I protested, knowing full well that I had read and re-read the packing instructions numerous times. However, despite what I had been directed to do by the RCMP paperwork, I was told by the airline staff member that under no circumstances could I board the plane with my baton in my carry-on. Confused and upset, I was informed that, to adhere to policy and to board my flight, I absolutely must place the baton in my now already-checked baggage. Stressed, I sprinted down a floor to the checked luggage area. Fortunately, I caught up to my bags just in time and hastily placed my baton inside, questioning the whole time what the proper procedure really was. Sweating profusely, tears once again streaming down my cheeks, I finally made it through security. I cried for hours as I left behind my home, everything I knew, and everyone I loved. I felt truly alone.

Many hours later and full of apprehension, I landed in Terrace, B.C., to a dark, dreary, rainy, and unwelcoming northern night. My RCMP trainer, the member assigned to coach me for the next six months, picked me up at the airport and drove me the forty-five minutes to Kitimat, making small talk the whole way. As we descended the long hill into the town of Kitimat, population approximately 10,000, he pointed off slightly to the left. There were three faint lights. "That," he said, "is the mall." Welling up for about the thousandth time that day, I stared in disbelief. "Seriously?!" I thought. I'm from a town of only 20,000 people, but this seemed very small indeed!

Trying to hide my dismay, I focused on trying to get my trainer to see me as being excited and keen. I so desperately wanted to project competence and confidence and enthusiasm, but I was exhausted and nervous, emotional, and questioning everything. I stared out the window, tears once again streaming down my face. I was willing them to stop, internally beating myself up for being weak, showing vulnerability, especially so soon after meeting him. Any trace of makeup was long gone. Forlornly, I avoided eye contact while pretending to be captivated by my new surroundings, awe-struck by the scenery, even though I couldn't see much of the mountains in the darkness. My trainer politely asked me if I wanted to go to a pub for a drink, but exhausted, I declined.

He then proceeded to drop me off at a sketchy motel, with dated orange and brown shag carpet and a dark, dingy kitchen. I curled up alone on the gross upholstered couch, looked sadly out the window at the town that was supposed to be my new "home," and began to sob uncontrollably. "What had I done to my life?" I thought, as I watched the rain hammer the parking lot.

Graveyards

Days later, I moved into my tiny rental apartment and began working. Two months into my duties, a new shift rotation began a trial phase in Kitimat, and I was scheduled to work straight nights. Yes, *straight* nights! No day shifts. Shifts began at either 5, 7, or 9 p.m.

I had no social life, so the gym became my only predictable off-work activity. It was a sad and lonely existence, peppered with very infrequent outings with work-related friends. I didn't have much opportunity to cultivate new friendships, so work friendships were all I had.

One day at the gym, I was minding my own business when a cocky, arrogant man swaggered up the aisle towards me, looked me from head to toe and back up again, gave me an approving nod, and said, "Hey!" I quickly turned the other way, anxious to steer clear of him and his obvious intention to strike up a conversation. He followed, oblivious to my reaction and said, "So, you're the new cop in town, eh?" I simply nodded, preoccupied with avoiding further interaction and focused only on creating some distance. He continued, "I'm Kevin. We should go out one of these days."

"Um, I don't think so," I muttered awkwardly and hastily turned in a different direction. I was taken aback at his gall. I mean, he didn't even ask for my name or try to have a conversation leading up to his suggestion to get together. It was odd, unnatural, and highly uncomfortable.

Fortunately I trusted my instincts and wisely declined that first awkward pick-up offer, because not long afterwards, after having been kicked out of that gym for offensive behaviour towards women, that man shot four young local men from his new gym, killing three and gravely wounding the fourth. He disappeared the day of that tragedy and, despite the massive search that followed, as well as being featured on *America's Most Wanted,* he has never been seen since.

Months later, we were out chasing kids during night shift. They were noisy, disruptive, and causing disturbances, and our dispatchers were receiving numerous complaints about their behaviour.

We entered the neighbourhood where they were wreaking havoc and I watched from a distance as a colleague jumped out of his police vehicle and began chasing the kids on foot. They were scattering in every direction and that, combined with the fact that I loathe running, made running around under those circumstances a very unappealing and ineffective approach. Instead, I drove up on the sidewalk in my police car and pulled up beside the main instigator who was still attempting to flee from us. I recognized the youth and knew he wasn't a true troublemaker, but I had no grounds to arrest him. However, *he* didn't know that, so I rolled down the window, looked at him sternly and ordered, "Get in the back." He glanced up at me, looked around for his friends, gave up when he couldn't see any of them, and grudgingly opened the back door of the police car. Deflated, he got into the back seat.

People are not mind-readers, and we cannot assume they know why or what we want. I have learned that being direct, and being my own advocate, is the most effective way of getting what I want. While I may not always be successful when I ask someone to do something, I am often surprised at how frequently I get exactly what it is I wanted.

Once, when I was on a boring summer night shift patrol, I was called to a disturbance at the only gas station open all night. This gas station had a sandwich bar, an ice cream bar in the summer, and was basically a hub of activity, should there be any nighttime activity at all. When I was dispatched, I was prepared for the drunkenness that usually accompanied such late night disturbances. As I drove up to the gas station, I heard very loud thumping coming from the rear of the store, near the dumpster. Knowing there was a pathway behind the store that led to a nearby residential street, I drove quickly up behind, adrenaline pumping, fully expecting to see people scurrying away. Instead, despite the darkness, I saw nothing. There was no movement at all. But the loud banging continued. I noticed that a dumpster was shaking. Confused, I turned on my take-down lights on my cruiser to get a better look. As I sat there staring at the noisy dumpster, the lid suddenly lifted. From inside the dumpster, up popped a black bear wearing a large, plastic, overturned ice cream pail on his head. The melting ice cream was dripping down his face. Startled by the bright lights in the darkness, the bear clumsily, but hastily, jumped out of the dumpster and shook off the plastic container while lumbering his way down the pathway.

My heart slowed down as the realization of the silliness I had just witnessed began to set in. Laughing and shaking my head, I drove away. Hilarity can be found so frequently. Sometimes, like in this ice-cream-pail-on-head-brush-with-bear situation, the amusement is blatant. But I try to remind myself to find the goofiness in other, less obvious situations, too.

An ability to find humour is absolutely *the* most effective coping strategy for virtually anything. While heaviness in life is inevitable, I am committed to finding more things in life that make me laugh. *Way* more things.

For months I remained on that graveyard schedule and was rarely able to participate in activities I enjoyed—skating, curling, softball, golf. I was terribly lonely, a most unfamiliar feeling for me. After all, I had a big family, I was a social creature, and I was accustomed to being surrounded by many friends. I had always participated in several sports and activities and rarely declined an offer to do something. Even the jobs I had left in Brockville were all people-oriented. I was finding myself uncomfortably lonely.

I enjoyed my job immensely, but with no end to the gruelling work schedule in sight, I began to allow myself to consider leaving the RCMP. I started researching alternatives. Could I handle going back to school? Again. For what? Should I revisit becoming a full-time teacher? Take a post-graduate physiotherapy course? Was Kitimat "bad" enough to leave? Could I just quit and risk returning home without any sort of confirmed backup plan? Could I tolerate moving home again? At what cost, psychologically and financially? My mind was constantly preoccupied, and I spent a significant amount of time analyzing my organizational commitment, my future. Could I live with myself if I left the RCMP? Would I feel as if I had given up? Would others perceive my departure as a weakness? Worse yet, would *I* consider *myself* a failure?

After excessive what-iffing and mentally rehearsing every possibility I could dream up, I made a deal with myself. If, after a full year of service, things didn't improve, I would give myself permission to leave with no regrets. I would be able to hold my head high, knowing that I had given this career a year, a fair and full year, before making a final decision. No one, especially myself, could fault me for being "hasty" after a solid twelve-month stint. After all, no one could expect a young, single, active person to live any sort of fulfilling life while working constant graveyard shifts.

And so the time slowly continued to pass, a total of *ten* months in fact, creeping towards the one-year deadline I had imposed. Then the work schedule changed! I began seeing the light of day a little more frequently. I was able to become involved in a few community activities. I golfed a little.

I took up curling. I got to know some local youth by doing school liaison duties. It was a relief to be out and about during the daytime. I felt more a part of the community, and people found me approachable. I volunteered in community events and was beginning to feel a sense of belonging.

I was developing some meaningful friendships outside of work and I was forming solid relationships with my colleagues. I was developing confidence in my investigational skills. My community involvement was helping me adjust and my self-esteem even got a boost when I was asked to model in a local fashion show! My loneliness was starting to evaporate. I was having some fun. I was belonging.

And I stayed.

Reputations

Near the outset of my career, I was called into the detachment office for a closed-door session. There, I was presented with a notebook chronicling my off-duty activities—where I had been, on what day, at what time, with whom, what I was wearing. As it turns out, one of my colleagues had been advised that I was "crooked," that I had been seen doing cocaine at a party.

As a result, an undercover operation had taken place. Police resources from headquarters had come into town to do surveillance on me, monitor my activities. That undercover operation had revealed nothing untoward.

I was in complete and utter disbelief because I knew the origin of the comment. And I also knew why it had been made. I was shocked that the RCMP was willing to put thousands of dollars into an undercover operation rather than simply giving me an opportunity to explain.

That explanation was this. Some friends, including other members from my detachment, made wine at a local business. The owner of the business hosted a customer appreciation open house at his home. I attended. Also in attendance was a drug user/trafficker with whom I had had several negative interactions. He disliked me, and it was no secret. I had entered a living room at the party, and that man was in the midst of rolling a joint. I went outside into the yard and then left the party.

The user/trafficker told my co-worker he had seen me there at the party. He fabricated a story indicating I used cocaine that night. I have never used cocaine.

Simple.

But no one ever asked me directly.

After the significant background checks that precede acceptance into RCMP training, followed by months spent in Regina at Depot, had my character suddenly become so fundamentally questionable that I didn't even deserve an opportunity to explain the origin of this man's comments? Did his off-the-cuff statements carry more weight than mine?

Wow.

Although the matter died down relatively quickly, what was not lost on me was the lengths the organization would go to follow up on baseless accusations. While that experience took place in the mid-90s, and things have changed since then, what was also not lost on me was that I was disposable, possibly untrustworthy, simply because an unreliable and questionable character nonchalantly pointed an accusatory finger at me.

I realized how quickly and easily my reputation could become tarnished or, worse, damaged irreparably, without ever having a chance to defend myself. I learned how much weight a simple comment from one person's perspective, whether true or false, can carry.

Fishbowls

After I arrived in Kitimat, alone and nervous, and was placed on straight night shifts, I began casually dating a local man. We didn't have many opportunities to get together or to go out in public, so I was fairly certain few people were even aware of our relationship.

As it turned out, not so.

One Friday evening, I received a call from one of my managers asking me to attend the detachment for a meeting at 5 p.m. My shift did not begin until 9 p.m., and this had never happened before, so, naturally, I was apprehensive.

I stewed all afternoon and then attended his office at 5 p.m. as requested. The door was closed, reinforcing my fear that a serious discussion was about to ensue. I was instructed to hand over my firearm and take my weekend shifts off, and then I was advised that I had until Monday morning to decide between my boyfriend and my career.

Bewildered, I departed the office. My mind was frantic. Was there something I didn't know about my boyfriend? What could be so serious? If there was something I should know about him, shouldn't my co-workers or my bosses inform me? Be direct with me? Weren't we on the same side?

The problem was that we were not authorized to use RCMP databases for checks on potential friends, dates, neighbours, or daycare providers. It was against policy.

Granted, this experience is long in the past, but I fundamentally and wholeheartedly disagree with this policy. If the RCMP is going to pluck me out of a world I know and plunk me down in a tiny, unfamiliar community where I know no one, wouldn't my ability to make decisions in my personal life be slightly improved by being able to utilize those systems? I didn't want to fail. I didn't want to make naïve or uninformed choices. I had worked so hard, I made many sacrifices, and I most certainly wanted to keep my job. However, I was completely alone, working straight nights, going home after every shift to an empty apartment. I had no family within 5,000 kilometres. I had few friends. I was extremely lonely, and I knew I needed some quality of life, some emotional connection, some support. In order to be set up for success, wouldn't it be reasonable to use some of the tools at our disposal to help us adjust to our new surroundings?

I recognize that I signed on the proverbial dotted line committing to serving our national police force *anywhere* in Canada. However, some members have the built-in advantage of returning to communities in which they have pre-established social circles—family members, friends, acquaintances, former co-workers, allies. For those of us whose circumstances were vastly different, why couldn't we use tools available to better equip ourselves to make solid choices? Wouldn't we avoid at least some potential conflicts? Wouldn't we save everyone a great deal of stress by being allowed to do what we are trained to do—gather relevant information and make educated, wise decisions based on that information? While I fully respect that the policy argument is based on privacy and the Criminal Code, I feel that a process could be put in place that would allow us to gather information, under proper supervision, simply to avoid dangerous risks and embarrassment. After all, police are held to higher standards of behaviour, and operating in isolation, without the benefit of familiarity or trust, can be very tricky. Wouldn't establishing some sort of assistance be a reasonable, helpful, and perfectly justifiable way of assisting us in positively establishing ourselves in our new communities?

After much soul-searching during my unexpected time off that weekend, I decided to question the decision, being forced to make a choice between my job and my boyfriend, because the truth was, I didn't know the true nature of management's concern. I pushed back, and in the end, after many sleepless nights, worrying if I was doing the right thing, I guess I "won" that battle. Management backed off. But there were costs. The romantic relationship was doomed from the start, but that hadn't been the principle. If in fact there was something I absolutely needed to know about my boyfriend, couldn't the information be shared with me in a non-adversarial way? Didn't my managers think I, too, would want to know?

What I learned was that I was now living in a fishbowl, and my position as a Mountie was one that was being carefully watched. My new role had put my actions under a microscope, and every decision I made, every social interaction I had, personal and professional, was going to be scrutinized. That scrutiny would lead to judgment and criticism. That was my new small-town reality.

Part 2 –

Upheaval

Ambushed

In 1998, two-and-a-half years after my arrival as a new RCMP constable in Kitimat, I began investigating an alleged sex offender. Because I was one of very few female members in the detachment, and because I had developed a keen interest in sex crime investigations, these kinds of files would often land in my in-basket.

In September 1998, the suspect had been charged for sexual interference on a file I was investigating, and he was due for his first appearance in the local courthouse. Initially, there was only one victim; however, word travels quickly in a small town. When others heard about the original victim's disclosure and her circumstances, additional victims became more willing to come forward about their own experiences with the suspect. Some of the victims took comfort in knowing they were not alone, and as a result of the momentum of the investigation, additional disclosures were made. The investigation became more complex in the weeks following the suspect's first court appearance, and ultimately, the same accused man was set to be arrested on subsequent sex-crime charges in November of that same year. At the time the planned arrest was to be effected, a search warrant for possession of child pornography was also scheduled to be executed on his residence.

On November 27, 1998, I, along with two other members, attended the accused's residence. His car was in the carport, but we were not sure if he was home. We knocked. No answer.

There were preschool children playing nearby, so we decided that we would contact the townhouse complex superintendent to obtain a key. The suspect didn't have a history to support a harsher approach, and a softer entry would be far less dramatic for the young neighbourhood kids.

The superintendent provided us the appropriate key for the suspect's unit, but when we tried it, the lock wouldn't budge. It seemed to be the correct fit, but the door simply wouldn't unlock.

I was under the carport standing to the right of the door, while my one partner was to the left. Our third partner was at the rear door of the residence.

I stepped back, planning to take the door key from my partner to the rear of the residence so we could try it in the backdoor lock.

It was a beautiful, brisk, sunny, late fall afternoon.

And that is the moment my life changed forever.

The unthinkable happened.

I was shot. Through a door. There had been no warning. I hadn't seen anyone. I hadn't heard anyone. I only heard the "POP." I saw the hole in the door. I smelled the gunpowder. I saw the smoke. I felt the excruciating, fiery, hot pain. My ears were buzzing, and I had an eerie sense of detachment while I was lying in a rapidly growing pool of blood. *My* blood. I was conscious and I was disconnected but I was acutely aware of everything going on around me.

Chaos was ensuing. I heard sirens. I heard urgent police radio messaging. I heard "10-33." Officer down. Emergency.

My partner knelt beside me and assessed my injury. "One bullet wound to the leg" was the report given to me and to the police radio dispatcher. My partner grabbed my clothing at the back of my neck with one hand and the waist of my gunbelt with his other hand. He dragged my limp and uncooperative body a few feet away so I could be better protected from further injury. I was near a green car in the driveway, under the carport, near a support pillar.

Two paramedic/firefighter friends arrived on scene and raced determinedly onto the pavement to rescue me. With no hesitation, no concern about the danger they were running towards, they rushed to my aid. They quickly picked me up. One wrapped his arms under my armpits, the other grasped me under the knees, and then they sprinted, carrying me to the waiting ambulance. As they raced with me, I saw a looming ditch and I worried about how they would transport me over it. Without even slowing down, they leapt across it with what seemed like superhuman powers. To them, in that moment, it wasn't an obstacle at all.

My body was limp in their arms, and I had no muscular control. I felt my right leg dangling awkwardly, my lower leg seemingly hanging onto my body by a thread. It was all so surreal.

The ambulance rushed out of the neighbourhood, sirens blaring, and when I arrived at the Kitimat hospital just minutes later, arrangements were already being made to fly me to Vancouver. I knew then that my situation was bad. *Very* bad. Only serious cases were transported to Vancouver.

In anticipation of the warrant execution and the likelihood of my crawling around searching the residence, I had opted that day to wear my own comfortable athletic clothing (along with my Kevlar vest and duty belt). I knew it would be less restrictive for me while I seized computer equipment and other evidence. I had left my RCMP-issued general duty uniform at home.

The flurry of activity around me in the emergency room was distracting, but I was very aware that someone was approaching me holding a large pair of scissors. Piece by piece, my clothes were cut off.

Rrrrip. There went my $60 Nike athletic pants.

Rrrrip. There went my $30 Club Monaco sweatshirt.

Rrrrip. There went my $20 Gap T-shirt.

My brand new $130 Merrell hiking shoes were covered in blood.

All I could think of was how much I regretted not wearing my uniform, that no one was being respectful of my clothes. Did they really need to wreck *everything* by hastily cutting everything away?! Did they know the value of the items I had been wearing?!

At the request of hospital staff, I dutifully removed my rings from my fingers, and found myself wondering who would be responsible for them. One ring was my grandmother's wedding band, and it held great meaning. My mind was jumping all over the place, and although I was able to follow instructions and answer questions, I felt very distant, very removed from the hospital room. It was as if I was watching the scene unfold from afar, yet oddly able to comply with commands.

Someone asked for my parents' phone number in Ontario, and like a good little emergency room patient, I obligingly chirped it out. Then, in a moment of seeming clarity, I offered up Lorelei's phone number. After all, she was posted in Coquitlam, B.C., and naturally, if I were suddenly going to be flying to Vancouver, she could probably meet me. "It would be nice to see her right now," I thought. "It's been so long."

I felt as if I were an object. I was surrounded by drawn faces, pursed lips, narrowed eyes. Those faces seemed white, devoid of any natural colour. People not directly involved in my unfolding medical care seemed fidgety, stand-offish, watching intently, not knowing what to do. Then a colleague who had not been at the shooting scene with us rushed into the room. She was very pale, and sheer panic was written all over her face. "Laurie, Laurie … do you have any dying declarations?" she asked. Bewildered, I tried to register the question … *dying… dying.* I slowly shook my head, trying hard to remember my law lessons from Depot. What exactly was a "dying declaration"? More importantly, why did she use that phrase? Was her choice of words significant? Was I dying? Do people die from gunshot wounds to legs? Was I so preoccupied with my injured leg that I was unable to register other injuries I had sustained? Suddenly overcome with fear and dread and panic, I patted down my chest, my torso, my stomach, wondering if I had been shot elsewhere too. Was I simply unaware of other injuries? I looked at the blood and the tourniquet on my leg and kept patting my body, but I couldn't find any other bullet holes. Confused, I lay wondering about that question, trying to absorb what was happening, trying to reconcile the intensity of the pain I was experiencing.

In those next few moments, I slowly came to a most terrifying realization. An idea began to bounce around in my brain, but I tried not to let it take hold. As I lost my capacity to control my thoughts, I mentally retreated further from that room.

"I'm dying," I concluded. "Everyone is avoiding direct eye contact, so I'm dying and no one wants to be the one to tell me."

As arrangements were being made for my departure from Kitimat via air ambulance, I remained conscious. My senses remained heightened, and the noise around me was almost unbearable. Everything was magnified. Hospital noises were intolerable. People's voices were far away, becoming increasingly tough to comprehend.

The man I was casually dating (a firefighter/paramedic, but not working during the shooting) had been contacted, and when he arrived, I felt an instant sense of relief. He brought with him a reassuring physical presence and much-needed comforting hug. I needed his face to be close to mine so I could focus on something other than the pain. I needed his hand to squeeze so I could assure myself I was still present. I needed to watch him closely so I could prove to myself I was still alive.

As the drugs began to work, and shock from the trauma and extensive blood loss took over, haziness continued to creep in. I was tired, so very tired. Everything was heavy. I felt like I was floating on thick gel, but the gel was slowly overcoming me, and my body was being pushed below the surface. My eyelids felt like weighted blankets. Blinks became monumental feats of strength and were executed in slow motion. My breathing was slowing down with every inhale. My body parts felt immovable, weighted down by cement blocks, and I couldn't fend off the smothering gel. I was cold. So cold. Yet my leg burned fiercely. It was a full-blown inferno.

I became weaker, and weaker still. The pain was excruciating. My leg burned, and I was desperate for the fire in my shin to be extinguished. That pain was pain unlike anything I had ever known; it was raw pain, right in the very core of my being. I realized I was slowly losing consciousness, but I was valiantly trying to fend it off and stay awake. So many times, I made myself blink slowly and deliberately, focusing on my boyfriend's face, trying to prove to myself I was stronger than this, that I wouldn't surrender. Panic was setting in, although I was trying with all my might to hide it and I wouldn't have been able to form words anyway. I was frightened beyond comprehension. But I simply *couldn't* give in. I *had* to maintain control. I *had* to fight somehow. Since my body was continuing to be absorbed into the gel, all I could do was will my eyes to remain open; that was the only thing I could still control. Sort of. They kept closing and each time they did, I would have a stern internal talking-to and force them open. I kept thinking about how much I wanted to see my parents before I died. I knew I couldn't let go because letting go and relinquishing my body and my mind to the gel, to the crushing weight of the cement, and giving in to the searing pain meant losing. Allowing the drugs and shock to take over, meant that I would never, ever wake up.

And even in the shock and the haze, that thought was incredibly alarming.

After four long, increasingly unbearable hours of fighting, I finally succumbed to the shock and the tremendous blood loss. I lost consciousness.

"Amputated ... "

I awoke in Vancouver General Hospital after a marathon eight-hour surgery. Desperate for the comforting faces of my parents, I wondered if I were home in Ontario. I groggily asked, "Am I in Ottawa?" I learned that my parents were still en route to Vancouver and had not yet arrived. So the boyfriend who had so graciously accompanied me on the air ambulance flight was left to deliver the life-altering news.

He held my hand and rubbed my hair while he searched for words. His eyes were bloodshot, his hair was disheveled, and he was clearly over-whelmed. He stumbled trying to figure out what to say. But there were no words that could adequately soften the blow from the message he had to share. I can't even recall how he finally phrased it or which specific words he chose. I just know that the only word that kept resonating in my foggy brain was "amputated."

"What?" I thought incredulously. "Amputated?"

I was still reeling, trying to absorb that news, when the surgeon appeared. He welled up when he explained that damage from the gunshot wound had been so severe that he had been unable to reconnect the circulation to my foot. The bullet from the sawed-off .303 rifle had struck me in the right shin approximately five inches below my knee. That type of bullet has a mushroom effect upon contact with a hard object, and as it struck my tibia, it split into a million pieces. The bullet had shattered both my tibia and fibula (the two lower leg bones between our knees and ankles), and the force of the fracture and the bullet exiting my leg essentially took my entire calf muscle with it.

Hazy, weak, and terrified, and seeing drawn, pale faces around me, I was told that in order to save my life, my right leg had had to be amputated. There was no other choice, and despite the eight hours of surgery, restoring circulation simply couldn't be done. Several surgeons had worked on me in the trauma unit, but my lower leg was gone. It was *gone*.

Overwhelmed and in disbelief, I couldn't grasp that concept. I was confused and scared shitless. Naively, I thought to myself, "Wasn't amputation associated with extreme violence in war-torn countries? Surely, it doesn't happen here in Canada where medical technology is so advanced."

The gravity of my situation was still lost on me.

But it was true. The sheets covering me couldn't hide that there was nothing there ... no foot, no ankle. My lower right leg was gone, but I couldn't look.

Oh my God.

To further complicate things, my left leg had a massive wound stretching from my inner knee to my groin where, before the final decision to amputate was made, the doctors had systematically and methodically removed chunks of a large inner thigh vein and transferred those pieces to my right leg in attempts to re-establish circulation to my right foot. Those valiant efforts to save my horribly injured leg and restore its circulation had left a huge, angry-looking, gaping surgical wound, haphazardly held together by numerous large, barbaric-looking staples.

What would I do with one leg? Would I walk? Would I drive? I'm a police officer. How will I support myself? What kind of career can I have now? I'm young. I'm athletic. What will my life become? I closed my eyes in utter disbelief. I just couldn't face the physical reality.

And the pain: the pain was excruciating.

When my parents finally arrived, I was instantly overcome with emotion. I couldn't have felt more relief to see their faces. They looked so tired, sad, drawn, and the stress they were experiencing was written all over their faces. It was virtually palpable.

As it turned out, my parents had been in Ottawa for a friend's birthday party when they had learned of my shooting. My younger brother, Steve, had been at the family home awaiting pickup from his friends; they were going away to watch football for the weekend. When a vehicle did pull up, it wasn't Steve's friends; rather it was the Ontario Provincial Police there to notify my family of what had happened to me in B.C. That is how my family received the news.

Steve tracked down my parents in Ottawa, and from then on, my parents were in touch with doctors in Vancouver about the ongoing progression of my surgery. At first, my parents were under the impression that I merely sustained a "flesh wound," but as the hours went on, my status became more and more grave.

On that same evening, my two Brockville-based brothers, Dave and Steve, and their wives, Les and Amy, sat around my parents' kitchen table looking at each other, wondering about my fate, waiting for the phone to ring with periodic updates from Vancouver. My other brother, Rob, arranged to fly to Vancouver from his home in New York. Lorelei arrived. My troopmate and close friend, Brad, flew in.

Although those hours were a blur for everyone, the situation was clear: I was a patient in the intensive care unit of Vancouver General Hospital, and I was an amputee.

Taking Things for Granted

While I was in the intensive care unit, I clearly remember lying in a very dimly lit room. I was hooked up to several monitors beeping in the darkness. I was receiving high doses of painkillers. I was fatigued beyond comprehension.

And I couldn't breathe.

My oldest brother was there in the room with me, peacefully holding my hand.

I looked at him, overcome with fear.

I couldn't breathe.

I truly believed my time on earth was done. I was finally going to succumb to the trauma, to the extensive blood loss, to the damage caused by that gunshot. I had escaped it on November 27, 1998, but now, a mere few days later, death was inevitable. My chest was heavy, so heavy. My lungs were immovable as if they were caved in, deflated from pressure. I told myself to breathe, wondering in my haze why I had to have that internal dialogue, why I had to *ask* my body to do what it had always faithfully done. But my body was not cooperating. It was not responding to my unspoken commands. I realized it was signalling to me that it simply couldn't take any more trauma. It was tapping out.

A tear slowly formed in my left eye as I looked at my brother, staring, not blinking. I couldn't breathe and I couldn't blink, two functions I had never before questioned. And in my mind, I told my brother I loved him, and I willed him to convey that love to the rest of my family. I was saying goodbye.

Moments passed; I have no idea how long. But then from somewhere deep down, I found the tiniest bit of strength. Maybe it was kick-started by the awareness of that single tear slowly gliding wetly down my cheek. I know the strength wasn't physical strength, as that had long been depleted. Maybe it was sheer willpower? Maybe it was my stubbornness, a result of a flat-out refusal to go, an unwillingness to accept that my time was up.

There was no way I was going to make it this far and give in now. How could I sustain a bullet wound, an amputation, tremendous trauma, yet slowly fade off a matter of days afterwards? I willed myself to breathe. I concentrated on activating my lungs, my nose, my mouth, to open, to draw in the smallest amount of air. I kept concentrating, visualizing my heart and my lungs and trying to remember the body's steps that take place during breathing. Ever so slowly, with a level of mental and physical commitment I had never experienced, I was able to get a single shallow breath.

In that moment, I realized that I was not entitled to anything in life, even breathing. Breathing is a gift. And I had to fight for the right to retain that gift. Since then, I have not taken anything for granted. That day, I had an epiphany; I realized that even the most basic, most fundamental physiological acts performed by our autonomic nervous systems, are privileges, not rights.

A highly skilled trauma team, along with thirteen blood transfusions, had saved my life. (In honour of that, and although I frequently flunk the pre-donation iron test and am subsequently rendered unsuitable for donation, I still give blood regularly. It's easy. It's free. It's important. I will continue making these small, yet meaningful, contributions, and I beg you to consider doing the same.)

A media circus ensued. Understandably, a young, female RCMP member gets shot in northern B.C. while attempting to execute a warrant on an alleged sex offender—that's headline-worthy. I had become high profile in a most unenviable way. Worse, she loses her leg, so my story had instantly become a powerful human-interest story for the Canadian public. The high-profile nature of my situation meant that the next several days were filled with a rotation of family and friends, colleagues, and other supporters. Along with family and friends, members from other police departments and government agencies came to show their support.

I was an amputee. And I was fighting for my life while the country watched.

In the Public Eye

While in the hospital, I was in and out of sleep, taking painkillers as often as my schedule allowed. Because of the extensive media coverage about my shooting, I ended up being inadvertently put in the position of playing hostess in my hospital room. In between naps, I halfheartedly held court for my visitors, bravely trying to keep a smile on my face for their sake. Visitors were arriving from everywhere, and letters and messages were coming in from all over North America. I was not courageous enough to look at what was left of my leg, so all of these distractions delayed facing my reality. As exhausted as I was, I felt strangely grateful for those distractions.

I was inundated with flowers, messages, gifts, visitors, and monetary donations. People sent art and knit sweaters. Family, friends, colleagues, and strangers all pulled together to support me. Considering there was no social media, and many people didn't even have cellphones, it was an incredibly impressive effort! As a country music fan, a gesture that boosted my spirits one day was receiving a phone call from one of my favourite singers, Lorrie Morgan!

I received cards with funny pictures from children in Kitimat; one read, "They should make bullet-proof pants!" Another poignant one had a drawing of a tombstone for the man who shot me. Among other things in the picture, the grave had no flowers beside it because the child artist clearly didn't feel the "bad guy" deserved them after what he had done to me. One friend sent me the most massive basket of Purdy's chocolates that I have ever seen!

Well-intentioned visitors brought self-help books and thoughtful collections of motivational, inspirational essays, but I could find no consolation in the words. I would halfheartedly pick one up to search for solace and comfort, but I would just sigh and quickly toss them aside. The words seemed silly and often trivial. The sentences and concepts seemed pointless and often patronizing. I loathed them and rolled my eyes at their insulting attempts to convince me to look on the bright side, to be grateful, to find meaning and positivity. I was *angry*. I wanted to be *allowed* to be angry. I didn't want to be made to feel *guilty* for being unable to find anything good about my situation.

During the seemingly endless hospital visits, at times I found myself consoling my visitors. It felt so odd; they felt inadequate, didn't know what to say, so I felt responsible for trying to fill up the airtime with chitchat. I tried to put them at ease with feeble efforts at being humorous, lighthearted, witty.

Between drug-induced sleeps, or even episodes of faked sleep in an effort to avoid conversation, I would shoot myself up with morphine, then stare longingly at the wand in my hand, willing the time away so that I could receive my next dose. I would press the red thumb button over and over in hopes that I had miscalculated the timing since my last fix. At the very least, I could hope for the tiniest amount to trickle down early, but it never did. It didn't matter anyway because it didn't feel as if the meds helped much, if at all. The button-pressing simply helped me feel as if I were actively controlling some little thing in my shattered existence.

Then I gave a press conference. I felt obliged to do so, despite my circumstances. After all, my situation was very high profile and so many people had shown support; it was only right that I publicly express my gratitude.

Press conference from Vancouver General Hospital.

Flowers and Compliments

In my haziness in those early morning hours in hospital in November 1998, I recall looking up and seeing a massive flower arrangement enter my dimly lit room. I couldn't see a face; it simply looked like an enormous flower arrangement being carried in on human legs.

It was a confusing sight, and as it drew closer, I saw the familiar yellow stripe of RCMP-issued pants and my troopmate's turban poking out from behind the stunning floral display. In the dimness, all I could make out of him was his white teeth and wide grin. With a foggy, fatigued smile, I asked him how he could possibly have come up with flowers at that time of day. He went on to explain that he had just finished up investigating a break-and-enter at a flower shop in Burnaby when he heard the news about my shooting. Upon his departure from the flower shop scene, the store owners, pleased with his professionalism in handling their file, and sympathetic to the tragic news my friend had just received, wanted to show their appreciation to him, and their empathy for my situation, by giving him those beautiful flowers to bring to me.

Those flowers represented something so very simple, something that often goes unnoticed or forgotten. They represented kindness, empathy, a reminder of beauty, despite the darkness.

Years later, I was reminded once again of that same, simple, yet powerful message. The backstory was that in my first weeks as an overwhelmed and impressionable cadet in Depot in 1995, I came to know and quickly crush on a cadet in our "Big Brother" troop (a senior troop assigned to ours to show us the ropes). I had been elated to go out on a date with him during training and, although a romantic relationship didn't materialize, I was grateful for his friendship, and we had remained in touch intermittently over the years. Shortly after I moved to the Vancouver area in 2006, my new boss suggested I take a spot on a supervisory course being held just down the hall from my office. There had been a last-minute cancellation, and I could fill in. The first morning of that course, I was running late. (Anyone who knows me knows that I am perpetually late.) I burst into the classroom in a whirlwind, flustered, out of breath, and apologetic. I slid into the first available seat, hastily unpacked my pen and notebook, and looked up into my former crush's smiling eyes.

That day on course, in that classroom when I saw his face, I was taken back in time. I spent the first hour of the course distracted by old memories and curiosity as to what his life had become. At the first break in the schedule, he waited for me outside the classroom. As I nervously exited through the door, I saw his grinning face, and he hugged me tightly, saying, "You look just as beautiful as ever."

I doubt my old friend even recalls that day. But I do. I remember it clearly. I remember it because details fade over time, but the feelings that were generated, emotions that surfaced, are what I remember.

That simple comment in 2006 came at a time in my life when I was struggling with my confidence, my identity, my physical abilities, my future. That simple comment reminded me that maybe I *could* still be beautiful. *Maybe* I was.

That friend lives in a different province, and I never see him. However, I will forever be grateful to him for that moment, for his warm smile, for reminding me of something which, at that time, I was not able to see on my own.

When I think of both the flowers in the hospital and the "beautiful" compliment years later, I am reminded just how powerful small, seemingly minor gestures can be. I am reminded of how deeply those two experiences touched me. Those two friends reminded me that we often can't fix other people's situations. We usually can't do much to make another's pain subside. Sometimes we can't find the "right" words. Sometimes we can't find any words.

What we *can* do is we can bring flowers. We can provide a burst of colour, a bit of hope, in a dark time. We *can* offer a well-timed compliment that will never be forgotten simply because the delivery of those words took place at the most perfectly meaningful time.

Those two men never knew how memorable their actions were.

Rallying

During those early months, my family navigated their different roles, and there was always lots of activity happening around me. However, none of those efforts could help me escape the pain, the excruciating pain. The instant I was shot, pain became the enemy. The pain varied. It kept me guessing and consistently had me wondering how I could keep it at bay. Always, it was deep, to the core. It was sheer bone pain, unlike anything I had ever experienced, and much worse than I ever could have imagined. But at the same time, it was superficial in many areas. It was frequently phantom pain, an incomprehensible phenomenon in which my body felt pain in a limb that no longer existed. It was burning, hot, deep, shock-like pain. It felt as if someone was hammering nails into the end of my heel and toes. It was severe cramping, the feeling that my foot and calf were being contorted into unnatural positions. It was vise grips on my toes, pulling them away from my body. It was shooting pains up from the base of my foot. It was needles poking into my unsuspecting body. It was like a thick electrical cord or rope in my instep, like leather stirrups being aggressively and torturously pulled straight upwards. It was at times unpredictable and sudden shock-like jolts. My body would tense up and remain stiff, dreading the next wave. Other times it was unrelenting and lasted for hours. It made me want to pull my hair out of my head. The morphine drip was nothing but a game, a game in which there was no winner. I would watch the liquid, pleading with it to give me a bit of relief, hoping for just a little reprieve from my nightmare. Then, once I was off the drip, the phenomenon remained the same with the timing of pills. I would watch the clock tick slowly, reviewing my notebook summary of pain meds, anxiously awaiting the next dose. While these silly tricks occupied my time, the meds barely even took the edge off. I constantly longed for sleep so I could briefly escape the pain. But the pain persisted.

Just three days after my shooting, for my 29th birthday, my brothers smuggled rum into my hospital room, and everyone put on a happy-*ish* face while they sang to me. I certainly couldn't stomach any alcohol, but I appreciated the diversion efforts.

I was in a fog. I was sweating and unable to cool down, soaking my hospital gowns and bedsheets. I was so cold that there were not enough blankets to warm me. I was feverish and slurring words. I was faint, dizzy, weak, unable to keep my eyes open. I was itchy from the epidural and the variety of tubes in my body. My leg throbbed. Both legs were numb from their respective wounds.

In those early days, someone, while well-intentioned, informed me, "God doesn't give you more than you can handle." *Really*? So unbeknownst to me, I had demonstrated to God, with such unwavering confidence, that I was capable of toughing out such a shitty blow? Somehow, I was to reconcile that, from the entire population of human beings, especially those who were trying to help make the world a better place by arresting pedophiles, I had been mysteriously selected for this inexplicable torture?

Nurses and doctors referred to my amputated leg as a "stump," and when I heard that word used the first time, I cringed. It seemed so harsh, so final. My stump had become the focus of my life, and I loathed having to hear the offensive word, so to lessen the sting, my brothers had affectionately suggested "Staub." My nickname has always been "Rusty," and Rusty Staub was a famous baseball player—the silly nickname stuck.

Over the next weeks and months, I would experience many firsts; firsts I didn't want to learn. I learned how to wrap Staub in order to prep it and shape it as suitably as possible for future prosthetic-fitting purposes. I learned wound care and bandages and anti-infection strategies. I learned medical phrases and terminology about amputations and prosthetic devices.

My family members all had various means of coping. Dad was quiet and pensive, worriedly rubbing his eyebrows like only my dad could do. Occasionally, for a break from the stress, he would get a few minutes of respite at the casino, but the long and stressful days were aging him right before my very eyes. It was traumatic for him to be unable to fix my pain, and his worry was impossible to disguise.

My three brothers took on logistics: inquiring about benefits and entitlements, salary, and compensation; researching health care providers;

sourcing out city accommodations necessary for when I began rehab. They all supported me in countless ways: helping with personal hygiene, shopping for necessities, raising funds for my trust account. My sisters-in-law at home in Brockville were fielding incessant phone calls and providing updates to concerned family and friends and other well-wishers.

And my mom … my mom was my champion, my advocate, my supportive team manager. She was my strongest ally, my trusted comrade. She was ever the hostess, keeping busy liaising with hospital staff, politely engaging with the never-ending lineup of visitors and co-workers. She dutifully kept track of mundane daily necessities such as medicine, wound care, and upcoming procedures and appointments. She asked all the questions and got all the answers, as only my mom can do; her unique and selfless rapport-building style always elicits valuable information and leaves other people feeling heard. She was my biggest fan and constant companion. She was always the go-to person for me, and she truly bore the brunt of my response to my physical and emotional pain. I know that my being my, um … "authentic self," wore her down. She suffered through my pent-up outbreaks of anger. She suffered through my meltdowns of tears. She had to hug me through the turmoil and the grief. I know that despite their efforts to assist, all my family members felt helpless and inadequate, but I also know that my mom felt it most deeply.

I was touched that so many people were reaching out, and I was overwhelmed by the gestures of kindness. Yet in true Catholic-guilt fashion, I was torn. While I was grateful, I wanted everyone to disappear. I wanted them to leave me the hell alone so I could turtle from the world and suffer in private. I wanted to wallow in my pain and grief and misery, but the parade of people left me no time for that.

In those first few months, both while in the hospital and then out, everyone took on a role. One of my mom's roles was to diligently track the names of individuals and agencies that reached out to support me. She and I would argue about what were reasonable ways of showing appreciation and gratitude. She felt strongly that every person should be thanked individually and directly. I, on the other hand, did not. I feel that when people give, they give without expecting anything in return. I also felt that my circumstances at that time easily justified no direct acknowledgement from me. I believed that people would understand.

During those weeks and months, I had countless flashbacks to my childhood when Mom would insist that I handwrite a note to anyone who had given me a gift. Mom was unrelenting on this. After every birthday and Christmas, I was required to produce those notes, specifically referencing the nature of the gift that I had been given.

> "Dear Grandma and Grandpa … Thank you so much for the $10 you gave me. This year I am saving to buy myself a new figure skating dress."

Mom lived with me for the early rehab months, and I relied entirely on her, so I felt I had no choice but to concede to the thank you cards.

Mom would reference her detailed and lengthy lists of emails, gifts, donations, and cards. She would then draft a response letter and request my input on wording (because, after all, they were ultimately to be signed by me). Once she had my stamp of approval, she would carefully tick the recipient off her enormous list and head to the mailbox with the letter. She did this hundreds of times, and together, we (okay, she) tracked down and thanked everyone we could possibly name or identify. We thanked family, friends, and colleagues. We looked up and thanked strangers who had reached out. We thanked donors who were listed on the bank documentation. We thanked the doctors and nurses who saved my life. We thanked everyone we could possibly think of.

It was a labour-intensive task, much more so for her than for me. In my opinion, at the time, it was completely unnecessary. Don't get me wrong. I very much appreciated all the kind-hearted gestures by friends, family, and strangers, but my heart simply wasn't in it. I think thanking people simply gave us something to do that was tangible and meaningful. It gave us some structure, tasks to chip away at during the seemingly never-ending daytime hours.

Eventually though, I became very, very grateful that my mom pressured me into embarking on that process with her. I realized that taking control of very minor things and accomplishing small, measurable tasks in times of struggle can be extremely rewarding. It creates purpose. It is positive. It promotes gratitude. It creates opportunities for achieving goals. More notably and fundamentally, for the first time in my life, I truly realized the meaningfulness and the magnitude of such simple gestures. I experienced the profound impact those "thank you" gestures and notes have—maybe not so much for the recipients, but for me personally.

A Most Inspiring Role Model

On November 30, 1998, my twenty-ninth birthday was spent in the hospital. I was completely in denial about my situation, my reality. On that day, in through the grey door walked an impressive man, a man who inspired me from the moment his enormous smile filled my doorway.

Constable Les Yee had dreamed of being a Mountie since he was a boy. He loved the iconic organization and wanted desperately to join the police force he so revered. That dream finally came true for Les when he was in his early forties. However, shortly after having his dream come true, and being posted to Richmond Detachment, he was faced with devastating news. Les was diagnosed with cancer. In 1998, as a result of his cancer complications, his leg had to be amputated below the knee. Les was about three months post-amputation when he showed up in my hospital room in Vancouver General Hospital wearing tear-away trackpants, the ones with snaps all down the outside of the legs.

I had never met Les before, but someone in the RCMP had contacted him to offer some much-needed moral support. Les burst into my hospital room with an air of confidence that disguised the complexity of his own struggles.

And his smile! His smile lit up the entire place!

Les was talkative, upbeat, and engaging. He was beaming, passionate about doing a show-and-tell of his brand-new prosthetic leg. He was busting to share his excitement.

I, on the other hand, was *not* eager to share his enthusiasm. I was extremely reluctant to see his leg because I was still in denial about my own circumstances. I hadn't even looked at what was left of my own leg. I sure didn't want to see *his*! I was overwhelmed and caught up in deliberately avoiding accepting my own amputation. But Les gave me no choice. He *was* going to show off. He would have it no other way! He exuded positivity, and although he was small in stature, Les's personality was truly larger than life. He tore away his trackpants, showed me his new equipment, and gave me a rundown of his leg's technical features. He then told me, as a matter-of-fact, how determined he was to pass the P.A.R.E. (the RCMP physical test) and get back to work. He actually *wanted* to do the *dreaded* P.A.R.E.!

Despite my personal hesitation about the prosthetics, I was struck by Les's positive attitude and in absolute awe of his determination. I was inspired by his unwavering dedication, while simultaneously taken aback by his apparent acceptance of the turn his path in life had so suddenly and unfairly taken.

Over time, I couldn't help but buy into his enthusiasm. His keenness was contagious!

With Constable Les Yee & Linda McLaren, my physiotherapist (1999).

Les became a huge source of inspiration to me in the early days, as well as a dear friend over the following months. I had the good fortune of meeting his wonderful, supportive family and I had the privilege of spending time with him at rehabilitation.

The fact that two RCMP officers with artificial legs were training to resume duties was a unique human-interest story, and the media devoted some attention to us and our evolving friendship. We provided interviews and were nothing but optimistic that we would both succeed; we would work hard, regain our lives, and resume our jobs serving the Canadian public. We were focused and we were committed! We sweated and ran and jumped and pushed ourselves. My schedule was like clockwork because I had nothing else to do but rehab, no other responsibilities. On the days Les didn't make it to join me, I fully understood; after all, he had a wife and small children, other commitments, other health issues. I would shrug off his increasingly frequent absences as I couldn't truly comprehend the pressures he faced. I simply carried on, pushing myself with more weight reps and more laps.

Then, in October 1999, Les died.

To this day, I am unsure if I deliberately chose not to accept the extent of Les's illness and the havoc it was wreaking on his body, or if he was simply a master at disguising it. Maybe I was naïve. Maybe he didn't want to let on how serious his situation was, and maybe he was protecting me. Or maybe it was my own self-preservation because I couldn't bear to fully face his reality and his heartache. I'll never know.

At Les's funeral, there was a video presentation that he had been working on in the weeks leading up to his death. He had known he was dying, and the video was the most powerful, moving experience I had ever had. I watched through tears of awe and amazement, of pride and admiration, of sadness and helplessness. On the big screen, I watched Les's grin, and I watched him share his life and his devotion to his beloved wife and children. I was honoured to be in that room, witnessing such love and life, witnessing him say goodbye to his precious family on his own terms.

Les's zest for life, his drive and determination, and his ability to remain optimistic when faced with impending death made him one of the most inspirational people I have ever met. I will never forget how he faced every single day with courage, excitement and hope, and I cherish the life lessons he taught me in the short period of time I had the honour of knowing him.

While he was alive, Les never knew how much he inspired me, how much he motivated me, how deeply he impacted me when he burst into my hospital room and then became my training partner. But it is because of his example that I developed such a passion for helping other amputees, for trying to offer a little hope, a little empathy, a little humour, and a little motivation to those struggling. That truly is what is fulfilling for me and what makes me strive to be a better person. I am so very grateful that Les showed me what it means to make a difference for someone in a vulnerable state, to offer encouragement when someone is floundering, to listen when someone needs to be heard. And as much as I dreaded that stinkin' P.A.R.E., I appreciate the fire Les lit under *me* when he announced *he* was going to do it.

Thank you for so many things, Les. You've been with me every step of the way.

Facing Facts

After the initial trauma, I was scheduled to have another procedure only two days later. I was absolutely terrified to have surgery so soon after the original amputation; I was convinced my body couldn't take any more and I was certain I would not make it out alive. That procedure, along with three others that took place in short order, were intended to debride wounds, remove shrapnel and bone fragments, and stitch me up efficiently in preparation for longer-term recovery. It had been tough for emergency room doctors to close up the end of my leg due to the damage to my calf muscle, displaced shards of bone, and wayward bullet pieces.

During the third procedure on December 2nd, my eyes inadvertently fluttered open, and I found myself looking into the reflective, glass ceiling in the operating room. Despite the distortion, a combination of anesthesia and pain medication, unfocused eyes, and glassy, brightly lit, mirrored décor, I caught a fleeting glimpse of the butchered remains of what used to be my right leg. I hadn't had the guts to voluntarily look at it before, and seeing it now, against my will, was devastating. I quickly squeezed my eyes shut, praying I wouldn't remember when I truly woke up. But I did … and I still do.

I spent the next days in and out of sleep, struggling to find effective doses of pain medication. I never could.

I fainted repeatedly and was frustrated by the lack of consistent progress. One day I would be able to make a few shuffling, one-legged moves on a walker or get pushed around sitting up in a wheelchair; the next I would be exhausted and physically unable to get myself past a seated position in bed. My body was stiff and numb and uncooperative. My head was dizzy, and my brain was unfocused; it felt as if it was wrapped up, protected by the fuzziness of a thick chenille sweater. My back was still itchy due to the anesthetic and epidural. I had a catheter and a tube stitched awkwardly into my neck.

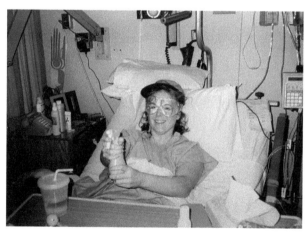

I was extremely emotional. I cried a lot. But I tried oh so hard to remain positive.

Pride

Like most people, I struggled with self-esteem during my teen years and early adulthood.

I was chubby off and on; my brothers seem to believe mostly on, while pictures don't quite support that to the same degree (although one school photo of me in a much-too-small, borrowed plaid shirt may substantiate their position). I had a lot of freckles, and there were no appreciable, distinguishable borders around them. I had red hair and, like everyone else with red hair, I was called "carrot top." My hair was a strange combination of very curly, wavy, and straight strands. I didn't learn about hair and makeup until well into high school, and even then, makeup choices and techniques that worked for my friends just didn't seem to work for me. I felt so strange putting dark mascara on my almost-invisible lashes. My brows blended into the skin of my pale forehead. Standard pink lipstick looked out of place on my face. I struggled with a curling iron and burned my forehead and tops of my ears often. I was very pale, almost translucent, so while friends would oil up and tan for hours, I would hide from the sun so I wouldn't burn and blister.

And those were just the physical things to stew about. There were other issues to beat myself up about too—I should be getting better grades, why am I not more quick-witted, stronger, faster, more this, less that. Self-confidence was an all-around challenge, and I felt as if I was average at everything. I mean, I wasn't terrible at anything (except maybe playing piano), and if I felt awkward at some physical task, like serving a volleyball, doing a layup in basketball, or throwing a softball, I would work at it until I was at least mediocre. But I really wanted to excel at *something*. I just didn't. I couldn't find that *one* thing, so I carried on, being … mediocre. I wondered why things seemed to come so easily to everyone else, and I was always worried about what other people thought of me.

When I finished my phys ed bachelor's degree and decided last minute not to pursue teachers' college as planned, I was very concerned about disappointing my parents. As a hasty consolation, I resolved to finish my master's degree in a year. When I successfully did that, I felt I was starting to come into my own. I was very pleased with the determination and perseverance my twenty-three-year-old self had shown in that accomplishment. Some of the self-doubt from my youth was subsiding, and I gave myself permission to be proud.

But that level of pride was nothing compared to the pride I felt on March 11, 1996. On that day, my graduation from RCMP training, I felt on top of the world.

I headed to my new posting and, despite my anxiety about my new role in the community, I was brimming with pride. *I* knew what I had overcome and accomplished to get there. *I* knew the dedication and the devotion I had demonstrated. I had earned it. I had proved to myself and everyone else that I was independent and responsible and capable and mature. Those PFO letters were a part of my history.

Yet a mere two years later, that pride, that dignity disintegrated into nothingness when my biggest accomplishment was ... having a bowel movement.

When you're in the hospital ICU, every move is monitored and recorded. The smallest, most insignificant events are viewed as huge (and sometimes embarrassing) milestones. If you have ever been in the hospital, you will know that when a person is trying desperately to regain some independence and freedom, and a ticket out of a hospital bed, pooping is pretty much the be-all end-all. No one talks about it, but it represents a monumental feat!

A gunshot had almost taken my life. The trauma and suffering had wreaked havoc on my body. Narcotics further compounded that havoc. My biggest challenge was to take a poop and have someone from the nursing staff vouch that I had actually completed that. After days and nights of medicine and constipation and catheters, it was suddenly and oddly exciting to have the sensation that I finally had to go to the bathroom! I mean, this represented a new step in healing and recovery and, more importantly, *leaving* the hospital. I was focused on achieving that sooner rather than later. I *had* to get out of there. The environment was stifling in so many ways, and so when I felt the urge to go, my youngest brother, Steve, was unfortunate enough to be the only other person with me in my room.

Laughingly, I told him I needed to go to "the bathroom." He looked at me with wide, round eyes as he realized what that meant, and a weird, but disgusted expression washed over his face. Clearly, he wished he could have been anywhere but there.

Weakly, and with his assistance, I sat up and then slowly positioned myself on my walker. He steadied me on my left, unstable leg, and slowly I made my way to the toilet. I was very dizzy, and my upper body felt like Jell-o. I would shift the walker a mere few inches in front of me and concentrate fully on dragging my left foot forward so it could be safely positioned to support me in my next lopsided step. Once my foot was placed underneath me, I would take a breath or two, lean on my shaky, rubbery arms, and do it again. My left leg wobbled, and not having the toe of my right foot to rest on the floor for balance was disconcerting. My arms weren't strong enough to support me well, and I was terrified they would give out. It was a painstaking trek to the toilet, but I was anxious to reach this new milestone in my recovery.

Finally, I was there. Exhausted from the strain of it all, I collapsed to sit on the toilet seat. I was sweating and breathing heavily. I hung my head, lightheaded, willing myself to stay upright, gripping the grab bar with all remaining strength. But the exertion of it all proved to be too much. Clammy from the struggle, I fainted while sitting on the toilet. Yes, my horrified brother had to rescue me.

I am still slightly embarrassed, but amused, by that story; however, I am also grateful that, despite the incredible awkwardness, it was a winning moment. Like graduation from Depot, it represented hope and a new start. It represented survival and perseverance. An obstacle had been overcome. It was a milestone in my recovery, and regardless of how insignificant it may seem to others or how it transpired, it was symbolic. I was on my way out of the darkest time of my life, and that's success. That's pride.

I learned then that not every milestone I achieve must be measurable by someone else's standards. Baby steps can be just as meaningful as quantum leaps, and progress is not always a continual upward trajectory. Sometimes, we are forced to tread water and focus simply on keeping our head above water. Maybe we will resume some momentum with an awkward dog paddle. And maybe, just maybe, there is a possibility of a full-speed front crawl. Measuring sticks are individual; they are not universal gauges of success, of productivity. They vary over time, and they range in scope. They range from bowel movements to RCMP graduations because success looks different in different circumstances. We owe it to ourselves to learn to take pride in every feat, every goal reached, every accomplishment, no matter how small or seemingly trivial.

Struggling to Cope

In mid-December 1998, I was released from the hospital. By default, Vancouver would have to be my temporary home because that was where the best rehabilitation resources were. Vancouver was going to be my new world, and I had to face my new reality as an amputee in a new city; it was overwhelming and terribly frightening.

But first, I needed some of my own clothes! I flew to Kitimat to collect some belongings and attended a detachment Christmas party. It was exhausting, yet familiar, to be back in my own apartment, around my colleagues and friends, and while the party was subdued given the recency of my shooting, it was a segue from hospital to the next phase of reality. After that, I flew to Brockville for a family Christmas. Because my shooting had been so high profile and my photos had been plastered all over the news, I was easily recognized at the airport. My wheelchair and redheaded one-leggedness were dead giveaways for my identity, so airline staff made every effort to make the flight to Ontario as enjoyable as possible. My mom, who accompanied me, and I were bumped up to business class, and the much-needed complimentary cocktails began to flow. The altitude exacerbated the throb in my giant, swollen stump, and the only remedy I could see was to take my meds on schedule and wash them down with as much booze as possible. Hell, we deserved it!

Hours later, we landed in Ottawa on a dark, wintry night. I was somewhat pissed, a combination of narcotics and too much booze on a weak, frail, beaten-up body. During that flight, we put in a good effort trying to forget the stress of the previous three weeks. Although the reprieve of having flight attendants wait on us was bittersweet and short-lived, it was a much-welcomed escape from my depressing hospital room.

In Brockville, in between wound care and meds consumption, there were many photo opportunities, interviews to give, relatives to see, and a few festive, welcome home parties to attend.

With Mom and Dad.

Through it all, I maintained an outwardly positive outlook, despite my painkiller-induced fogginess. I dutifully put on my makeup, styled my hair, pasted a smile on my face, and said only optimistic and upbeat comments in the media. It was a short respite from what had been and what was to come.

During these events, it was difficult to ensure conversation flowed, but my attempts were well-intentioned. I was tired of answering the same questions, yet I knew everyone was uncomfortably and awkwardly doing what they simply felt they should—just showing up and offering support. Showering and dressing were monumental tasks in those early days, and mundane daily routines were laborious and exhausting. Everything took far more time than it ever had before. Once I was finally showered, dressed, and had makeup on, I would perch on a couch and engage with the seemingly never-ending parade of guests.

My left leg was forced to become my only base of support, and I had no choice but to learn to trust it. I instantly became hyper-aware of my terrain—gravel, snow, ice, sand, and pavement. I carefully watched for transitions from tile to hardwood to carpet to throw rugs. I was acutely aware of the slipperiness of wet roads and snowy sidewalks, the uncertainty of my varying degrees of stability. Minor inclines and declines were enormous challenges, and all were very real fall hazards. I was extremely weak and off balance. I had to concentrate hard on every move, every placement of my crutch tips, ensuring that my body didn't dangerously under- or overestimate my propulsion to the next one-legged step. My muscles wouldn't function like they once had, and intervals between pain meds were far too long. The constant awareness and attention required for physical efforts absolutely exhausted me mentally. The physical exhaustion was even worse.

Why Me?

Naturally then, with the intense emotional and physical turmoil, I became consumed with the age-old dilemma of wondering, "Why me?" I spent countless wakeful nights, countless hours of countless days asking myself this question. Why did *I* get shot? Why did *I* have my leg amputated? Why *me*?

What I finally did conclude, at some ill-defined point along my journey, was that bad things happen to everyone, even good-hearted, well-intentioned, ethical people. Contrary to what I used to naively believe—that good things will always happen to good people and bad things will eventually come to those who deserve it—it is simply not true.

Some of the best people I know have had total shit thrown at them. I have had the privilege of knowing many incredible individuals who have experienced death and disease and suffering and loss to a far greater extent than I ever have and, hopefully, ever will.

Similarly, some of the worst people I have come across seem to coast through life relatively unscathed.

I admit that, from time to time when I am struggling, I still catch myself reverting to, "Why me?" After all, it is normal, and I believe that anyone who says they *never* ask that question when they are facing hardship is being dishonest with him/herself. We all do it to some extent, maybe not aloud and maybe not very often, but we do. I just know that as the years continue to pass, I am aware that I ask that question less and less often.

I no longer ask it as frequently because the simple answer is that there is *no* justification for why this happened to me. There is no rationalization. And even if I had an answer, it would not have changed my circumstances, *my* outcome. There is no adequate explanation and there will *never* be an answer that makes sense or brings peace. It simply is.

It has been suggested that there are five stages of grief, one being anger. So I feel fully justified in screaming, swearing, and having a full-on meltdown when seemingly unfair things happen. Immature or not, I do it and I encourage others to do it, simply for the release. After all, challenging, upsetting circumstances can rationalize those juvenile, yet cathartic, *Why Me?* reactions. But, after having that release and getting it out of our system, it is time to stop complaining. It becomes time to analyze options, solve problems, and move towards next steps. It becomes time to stop wallowing in the *Why Me?*

I have also learned that if I develop certain theories, certain sweeping statements about myself and my life, and if I phrase those theories in a negative way, I will, mostly unwittingly, search for evidence to support those stupid theories. For example, some of the unreasonable theories to which I have subscribed are:

- "I *deserved* it."

- "Life *is* unfair."

- "Everyone *is* a bad guy."

- "I'm destined for a life of unhappiness and suffering."

Those sweeping statements have often consumed me in low times, times of misery, despair, and sadness. As a result of arriving at these conclusions, and fully believing them while not questioning their validity, not looking at reality through a fair and reasonable lens, I let them define me. I subconsciously carved out a path, an existence, which was based on deliberately and intentionally sourcing out evidence to support these theories. It was easier to find things that helped them hold up, to allow confirmation bias to rule my thoughts. This way, I could get off easily. I could say, "*See*? I told you so. I *did* deserve it. Life *is* truly unfair. Everyone *is* a bad guy. Obviously, my theories are true because here are the facts, which can lead to no other conclusion."

Over time, fortunately, I have been able to redirect my thinking and reword my theories. I am better able to present them in a positive light. While work remains to be done in this area, and progress can be slow at times, I'm better equipped now. I'm able to allow myself permission to wallow briefly in self-pity, to ask stupid, unreasonable questions about why certain unfair things have yet again been thrown in my path. I'm better able to cope with, and manage, what I now know is a perfectly normal and natural phase. But I'm also better at more quickly rephrasing the useless *Why Me?* question. I can consciously change it into a statement of what is. I'm learning to actively shift my perspective and view negative things in a less judgmental, more rational and accepting manner. At the same time, I'm developing resilience by focusing on solutions, on modifying goals, on possible results.

Maybe someday I will even arrive at a truly evolved state where I can shrug and ask, "Why *not* me?"

Suicidal Thoughts

From the day I was shot, I have been in pain. Things just … hurt. Many things.

Some pain is constant, fluctuating in intensity, but constant.

Other pain comes and goes.

But on some level, there is always pain.

Initially, I was in excruciating pain from the gunshot itself; reminders of that torturous physical pain still make me shudder. Nothing I have experienced since even approaches that realm.

People ask me what it was like to be shot, to have a rifle bullet go right through me. It is so very difficult to describe. It was a burning, fiery, agonizing, indescribable pain. It was localized to my leg only briefly. It was searing, like what I would imagine a scorching flame to feel like. As the pain quickly spread through my body and shock took over that day, the pain seemed to take over the deepest part of my core. It became a raw and unimaginable pain in my soul.

After surgery, the anesthesia after-effects wore off much too quickly. The pain medications were largely ineffective, and because they couldn't do what I felt they should be doing, all I wanted to do was to sleep. To escape. But even sleep couldn't give me reprieve from yet another new and inconceivable type of pain.

Phantom pain is something that sounds unbelievable and is impossible to adequately explain. It sounds as if it is a psychological pain (and I was even told this from a few uneducated, non-medical sources in the early days), but I assure you it is physical pain in its purest form. To anyone who has suffered phantom pain, to be told that the pain is "all in your head" is both insulting and infuriating. My brain could never dream up such a hellish concept.

Phantom pain is experienced differently by individuals without limbs, and not everyone missing a limb does in fact experience it. It is pain that is not unique to people who become amputees at some point in their lives, but rather it may occur even in someone who is born without a limb.

I don't understand it, but the best way I can describe it is to think of your body as a pre-hardwired entity. Nerves and sensations and pathways throughout the body are already physiologically designated to do certain jobs. But when a limb is not there, either from birth, or as a result of surgery, the body doesn't necessarily comprehend that absence. Messages are constantly being sent from the brain, despite the knowledge that the limb is not physically present. No matter how hard we try, we have difficulty interrupting that circuit, even when the circuit is of no use. Frankly, this description, coming from me, a non-scientific source, does little to account for the reality of the intense pain it causes. But it is the best I can offer.

For me, in the early months before I acquired a prosthetic leg, phantom pain was unbearable. I felt deep, burning pain in my ankle, foot, and calf muscle. At times I felt like my foot was being violently twisted, caught in a terrible, contorted wrestling position from which I couldn't escape. Other times I felt horrible cramping that could not be relieved. Still other times I felt like my leg was actually on fire, yet the fire couldn't be extinguished.

My leg was incomprehensibly itchy. I had crazy, shock-like spasms that occurred both day and night. My whole leg would suddenly jerk off the bed or couch. My heart would instantly begin to pound, and the pain was short-lived but unpredictable in frequency. I would fear the next one, dreading the gripping shock that would inevitably return, hoping desperately it wouldn't, but knowing indeed it would. It was simply a matter of time. Seconds? Minutes? The uncertainty was agonizing.

In attempts to alleviate the pain, I drugged myself with cocktails of heavy-duty prescription narcotics. I arrived slightly over-medicated (ok, pretty much stoned) at my physiotherapy sessions more than once. I was sent back home to bed equally as often.

I tried mirror therapy, where a mirror is positioned in such a way that I could visualize my amputated leg engaging in muscle movements performed by my sound leg. I would try to scratch or massage or move my sound leg (in my case, my left), while simultaneously visualizing the same action occurring on my amputated leg. It didn't work. Besides, staring at my residual limb in a mirror simply made me feel overwhelming despair.

I tried wrapping my stump in a specialty fabric, which is woven with fine fibres intended to repel magnetic forces in the air. I wanted desperately to believe in the theory, but I don't believe it helped me much, if at all. I bandaged up my stump as tightly as possible, hoping that I could extinguish the pain by smothering it. That mostly produced a different pain by temporarily compromising my circulation.

The excruciating pain in my non-existent ankle and shin was a constant, unpredictable reminder of what I had lost. It was an unrelenting shock sensation that taunted me. I couldn't escape it. The feeling of loss was overwhelming, and it was constantly in my face. What I could no longer do far exceeded what I could still do. My future was bleak, and I saw no hope. Absolutely none.

So I contemplated suicide. Often.

For many weeks, maybe even a few months, suicide seemed like the only viable solution to a devastating situation. Initially, I had been grateful I had not died from the gunshot, and everyone and everything around me reinforced the messaging that I was *supposed* to be grateful to be alive. But I was *not* grateful. I was full of bitterness, hate, and misery. I was overcome with loss and grief. Though my mind was still hazy from the drugs and the pain, I was slowly grasping my new reality and starting to comprehend the magnitude of all the things I could no longer do. Day-to-day routines were mundane, and I began each morning filled with dread. All I could see was the bleakness of each long day ahead. The hours of suffering. The lack of interest in anything. I couldn't see hope, and I couldn't envision a future; to me, there wasn't one. Everything was gone, and I was immersed in inescapable emotional turmoil. I couldn't take the pain anymore and I wanted to die, to just disappear. I needed some sort of respite. After all I had been through, all I had endured, I deserved peace, didn't I? Suicide seemed like the only way out, the only way to find that peace that I so desperately craved.

I thought about suicide a lot. I thought about it during the day, and I lay awake at night wondering how I could quietly die without causing my family any more anguish than they had already endured. I was angry I had to continue to live like this, and I just wanted to go. I truly regretted that I hadn't died that November day. I wished that bullet had ended my life. If it had, it would have been easier; I wouldn't be forced to face this unbearable suffering.

I would lie around, looking at the various bottles of pain medication, wondering if they were a pathway to escape. Could I ingest enough so that I could kill myself? Could I end my pain by suicide? With an overdose? It seemed like the only possible method available to me, given my dependence on my mom, the availability of narcotics, and my lack of physical functioning and abilities.

My pistol had been secured in Kitimat, but the very thought of guns and bullets was sickeningly gruesome anyway. I certainly couldn't shoot myself; after all, a gun had caused all of this in the first place.

I didn't have much coordination and couldn't remain upright well enough to hang myself. That was not an option.

I was so mentally foggy and physically too weak to strategize, and fortunately, I was too ill-equipped to act anyway. I was so, so sad. It was a level of despair I had never before experienced. I had officially been kicked out of my life, a life I worked for and wanted. Now, I was nothing but a burden. I hated myself and I resented my circumstances, so the only reasonable option I could wrap my head around was to hope and pray that I could just fall asleep and simply not wake up. If I could just slip away, fall asleep, and never wake up, it would be best for me and for everyone. Every time I put my head down and tried to sleep, I hoped I would just fade off. I hoped that my body would cooperate and agree with my brain by recognizing and acknowledging what I knew – that I could not continue down this road. I wanted to give in to the trauma and the pain and the suffering. I prayed that I wouldn't open my eyes ever again – the same eyes that I had willed with all my might to stay open in the hours that had unfolded right after my shooting. Each time I did wake up, I would beat myself up, wondering why God hadn't shown me mercy. I would question why I couldn't muster up the courage to follow through and swallow those pills. Was I lazy? Worse, was I too mentally weak to follow through? The days dragged on. And the cycle continued.

I still cannot say what prevented me from following through. I don't know what stopped me on so many occasions on so many days, and I wish I had an epiphany to share. I don't. I just know that time and distance from that phase has shown me that I really didn't *want* to die. I just needed the pain to stop.

What I know now is that suicide would not have been an end to my pain. It would have only resulted in passing my pain on to those who love me. Maybe somewhere deep down, buried in my subconscious, I knew that then. Thankfully, killing myself was simply something I could not do.

So I lived.

I Deserve It

When I was in the early months post-shooting and seriously contemplating suicide, I was literally incapable of stopping crying. I was so grief-stricken and overcome with unrelenting psychological and physical pain that I was having trouble functioning. Fortunately, I realized the depth of my emotions and I sourced out a highly recommended therapist. I cried in the taxi to her home office, and I cried through the whole appointment, and I cried on the way back to my condo. I attended several appointments in virtually the same state. However, though I was desperate for help, I also became very aware that this therapist was pre-occupied with tasks such as distributing forgotten lunch kits to her children and allowing pets to go outside for bathroom breaks. Those kinds of home-office disruptions are understandable on an occasional basis, but their frequency and regularity reinforced to me that I didn't matter; that's the message I received. I was getting no help, I was struggling with low self-esteem, and I simply couldn't take it, so I quit.

But I knew deep down that I desperately needed therapy, so I persisted, and with a little more effort, and a lot more research, I was fortunate to find excellent care.

Self-esteem struggles aside, I now know I deserved good care back then and I am confident I deserve it now. I am worthy of it; I have always been worthy of it. Psychological health is often overlooked, minimized, pushed down our to-do lists. We make excuses; we dismiss it. In reality, we must shift our thinking, prioritize our mental health. We absolutely need self-care and that includes our brains, not just our bodies. Psychological health is critical for overall well-being.

Keeping My Dukes Up

When I was in the intensive care unit, my family had the unenviable job of trying to find answers to stark questions:

- How would I pay for expenses associated to rehab?

- How would I arrange for rent payments so I didn't lose my apartment in Kitimat?

- Would I still receive my regular paycheque?

- Would I go on some reduced salary, some sort of disability plan?

- What about the transportation expenses? I couldn't drive, so would I need to arrange for taxis or Handi-Dart accessible transportation to get to rehab and to buy groceries? If so, who pays?

- Will only certain portions of my prosthetic equipment be covered? Are there limits? Spending caps? If so, what are they?

After all, I hadn't even reached full constable status (that level is not reached until three years post-graduation from Depot), and arrangements were being made for me to move into a furnished condo in one of the most expensive cities in the country.

As my family members made inquiries, they struggled with receiving adequate answers, fact-based information. Their persistence around accessing basic policy information resulted in delays, inaction, and they were called "a bunch of rednecks who wouldn't take no for an answer." My dad was criticized for apparently not appearing to be "a tower of strength" in how he was coping with my trauma. It seemed that simply because I had been injured, I was suddenly now in an "us vs. them" situation with the system. *I* felt like the enemy.

Navigating unfamiliar territory during any stressful time is naturally highly emotional. To complicate that stress by not receiving answers in a timely manner adds unnecessary layers of frustration. Poor communication exacerbated an already tremendously trying time, and unfortunately, what that experience taught me was that, like in boxing training during Depot, I must keep my dukes up, to protect myself and to push back. Keeping those dukes up meant survival.

37 Steps

In January 1999, once the Christmas season had concluded, I moved into my new temporary residence in False Creek in Vancouver. My brothers had painstakingly chosen the location for me, thinking that the sea wall would provide a wonderful environment for me to relearn to walk. I had not actually been involved in selecting the condo, nor had I even seen it, and as my mom and I pulled up to my new address in a taxi, it dawned on me that the front door was up from the roadway. *Way up.* I counted the stairs. *Thirty-seven steps up!* My heart sank.

Discouraged and highly emotional, I awkwardly exited the cab. I stood there on my crutches, took a breath, and sighed as I began the trek up to my front door. I struggled up the mossy, slippery, wet wooden stairs on my crutches. Each step was a taxing physical challenge. My upper body muscles throbbed from the exercise. My left leg was protesting about the exertion from climbing thirty-seven steps. My mind ached from having to focus so carefully on each step. Exhausted from the energy expenditure, I finally arrived at what was to be my front door. I reluctantly entered my condo and turned down the hallway towards the small kitchen. Disinterested in my new surroundings, and full of sadness to be standing in a place I did not want to call home, I half-heartedly looked around. What caught my attention was a full-length, extra-wide mirror on the wall. That mirror was in the kitchen, in *my* new kitchen. I glanced at it and looked away, shocked at what I had seen. I slowly turned back towards the mirror, but what I saw in that reflection was unrecognizable. It wasn't me. It couldn't be me. It was a stranger. I didn't know the pale-faced, drawn, terrified amputee looking back at me.

But it *was* me.

I fired one crutch right at the mirror and the other across the room at the dining chairs. They loudly hit their targets and crashed to the floor. And I had a meltdown.

I sobbed for hours, tears streaming down my face, telling my heartbroken mother:

> "I *hate* myself."
> "I hate the way I look."
> "I hate my life."
> "I hate Vancouver. I don't *want* to live here."
> "Why did *I* have to get shot."
> "Everything is so *fucking* slow."
> "What will become of me?"
> "I'm so *fucking* angry!"
> "I should have died. I *wish* I had died."

I bawled, I yelled. I sobbed. I gasped for air. I swore and swore and swore.

Over the next weeks, depression, which was already my constant companion, worsened. Energy was virtually non-existent. I lay on the couch mindlessly watching TV, dozing off and on with little awareness of time. The condo had three floors plus a rooftop patio. The kitchen was on the main floor, two bedrooms and a bathroom were on the second, while the family room was on the third. Having to tackle several stairs simply to go to the washroom was daunting, and physically tiring, so instead of attempting to use my crutches, mostly I sat on my butt and shuffled across the floor and down the stairs. I would slide into the bathroom and propel myself up off the floor and onto the toilet seat, using hands and elbows and countertops and sides of bathtubs for balance. That most basic task, one that I had always taken for granted, had now become a monumental feat. I would reduce my fluid intake, and reposition myself on the couch to minimize pressure on my bladder, in hopes of avoiding unnecessary trips to the bathroom.

Healing was torturously slow. Wound care was ongoing, but I had to remain vigilant because the fear of infection was real. As slowly as I felt things were going, any extra redness, pain, or wound seepage could result in days or weeks of further delays. And despite our best efforts, infections did occur. When they did, it seemed so unfair, given our diligence. It seemed like further punishment for an already rotten situation. Setbacks were frequent. Everything hurt. My arm muscles hurt from the crutches, and my armpits were raw from the chafing crutch pads. My palms and fingers had callouses from the crutch grips. My left leg was overworked, and muscles begged for relief. I couldn't get comfortable during the day. Nights were worse. I had to have my stump elevated, propped up on pillows. Any time my stump hung down, the blood pooled in it, it became purple, and it throbbed like hell. My back ached constantly. I couldn't sleep restfully or restoratively. Medication seemed like a feeble attempt to provide relief because it barely touched the surface of the pain.

And that was just the physical stuff.

Psychologically, I had far too much time to dwell on all I had lost. I grieved for who I had been, who I used to be. I didn't know who I was anymore, who I could or would be.

Every single morning, I was filled with dread when I opened my front door. I would painstakingly tackle the thirty-seven-step descent to the sidewalk to start my day. Every single day, a few hours later, exhausted from the exertion of physio, and my new life as an amputee, I would stand on that same sidewalk looking up at those same thirty-seven steps. My heart would fill with dread as I looked up at my front door so very far away. I would slowly and carefully crutch my way up, collapse on the couch, and close myself off from the outside world.

Those 37 steps represented *everything* I despised.

Fostering Empathy

Months after my amputation, I was crutching along a busy street in Vancouver, practising walking as I did for hours every day. From about fifty feet away, a mother approached with her two young children. I watched the mother's eyes as she deliberately made no eye contact with me but instead stared directly at my prosthetic leg. She could not take her eyes off my leg. With every step towards me, her eyes didn't waver.

She finally passed me, and I was intrigued by this woman's blatant disregard for normal etiquette. Her stare had been so obvious. I turned around to see her bent down pointing at me and talking animatedly to her two small children. Interestingly, her two children had not even noticed me, but this adult woman had been compelled to make a spectacle simply because I use an artificial leg. Since they were stopped mid-sidewalk, four or five other people had also begun to congregate, and all were staring at me.

This mom had no impulse control and was teaching her children that it is socially acceptable to point, stare, gesture, and generally create a small scene. In fact, instead of teaching her children about respect, her behaviour was showing her children what segregation and divisiveness can look like. She chose to treat me like an object on display.

I understand the intrigue, that prosthetic legs are interesting, as are wheelchairs and many other pieces of equipment and hardware associated with certain disabilities, but our differences should not be highlighted in such public, shameful, even humiliating ways.

More recently, I was at the gym, and a gorgeous man hopped on the cardio machine beside me. I glanced up and smiled.

Right away he said, "So, how did you lose your leg?"

"Wow, mighty bold!" I thought to myself, while shaking my head.

In his defence, the prosthesis I was wearing that day had no cosmetic cover, nor had I made any attempts to disguise it or make it less obvious. However, his lack of social awareness, and his inability to think before speaking, was clear.

Unlike me, many people are *not* forthcoming or open about discussing their disabilities, and I could have easily met his question with embarrassment or awkwardness or anger. Maybe, just maybe, *I* would not be okay with addressing my disability with a stranger. Maybe my amputated leg was a result of cancer. Maybe I was born this way. Maybe it was the result of a tragic accident. Whichever way my (or anyone's) story goes, there is an inherently high likelihood that this kind of conversation could go sideways.

Don't be the insensitive parent who makes public spectacles of people with disabilities. Don't be the impulsive guy at the gym who blurts out questions simply to satisfy personal curiosity.

Instead, lead by example. Show some discretion. Discourage your children from staring and from judging others. Encourage them to be inclusive and allow their curiosity to evolve naturally. Teach your children to ask respectful questions. And do the same yourself. Be aware that a six-year-old can get away with asking almost any question. You, on the other hand, cannot. Adult rules differ, and they are not as flexible; expectations of tolerance change with adulthood.

Be better, simply so our kids learn to be better.

We need to foster more empathy. And these days, we need it *everywhere.*

Attitude Adjustments

Every Mountie knows what an "attitude adjustment" at Depot means; it is punishment for certain unacceptable behaviours. The nature of the "AA" could vary, depending on which instructor handed it out and which lesson he or she was trying to teach the cadet.

I was fortunate that I was never on the receiving end of an attitude adjustment at Depot, but I had most certainly witnessed them and their effectiveness at eliciting the desired change!

In January 1999, just days after moving into my condo, I was scheduled to begin rehabilitation at G. F. Strong Rehabilitation Centre in Vancouver. I was caught up in my own despair, both physical and psychological, and I very reluctantly pulled myself together the first morning I was scheduled to be there. Dutifully, I painstakingly readied myself. I showered on my bath stool with my handheld showerhead and my waterproof leg cover. I dressed. I ate. I brushed my teeth—all the things I always did. But everything took so long now, even the simple, most basic tasks. To make matters worse, I absolutely did *not* want to go. I wanted to be in hiding, to turtle from the world. Forever.

But despite my hesitation, and likely because I'm a rule-follower and I was scheduled to be there, I forced myself to go. I arrived at G. F. Strong angry, withdrawn, sullen, bitter, discouraged. Mostly, I was feeling sorry for myself.

I was consumed with destructive thoughts and self-loathing. "Why me?!" was all I could wonder. It resonated in my head thousands of times a day. My internal dialogue was all negative, interspersed with a great deal of sighing and grunting, and peppered with "Fuck!" and "This is fucking bullshit!" and "Holy fuck!"

As it turns out, what I didn't know was that *I* was in desperate need of a powerful attitude adjustment.

When I arrived that day at G. F. Strong, the facility's automatic doors opened up to a world I had never seen before. I was instantly overcome with the pungent, all-too-familiar hospital disinfectant smells. But instead of the familiar hospital setting I expected, my eyes opened widely to a much different scene. In front of me were several people of varying ages, in various states. There were crutches, canes, wheelchairs, hospital beds, intravenous tubes, and other life-sustaining equipment. There were burn patients, car crash victims, amputees, and stroke patients. There were people with brain injuries and spinal cord injuries. There were teenagers, there were people my age, and there were elderly folks. There were men and women.

I realized right then and there, that despite my losses, despite having almost died, despite *wanting* to die, despite having some significant challenges ahead of me, I really had no business feeling sorry for myself. None.

And that day I experienced *my* first truly powerful attitude adjustment.

Group Therapy

I began daily physio sessions, and during those appointments I was introduced to several other in-patients and out-patients. One of the social workers collaborated with my physiotherapist to orchestrate a support group of sorts, with two other women.

Heidi was in her early twenties and had been in a severe car crash. That crash had claimed the life of her dearest friend and left Heidi in terrible shape, with a coma, significant burns, and ultimately two below-knee amputations.

Gail was a little older than me and was battling cancer. She was a married mom and had had one leg amputated above the knee.

Despite our differences in age, in situations, in health issues and challenges, in amputation circumstances, we all agreed to participate in the support group. It was difficult opening up, talking about our fears, our losses, our individual medical issues, our frustrations, our never-ending, but necessary, adjustments to the day-to-day challenges we were each forced to face.

We shared, we cried, we raged. We felt sorry for ourselves and we felt sorry for each other. We took turns monopolizing the conversation and sitting in silence. We were present. We comforted each other and nodded empathetically. And occasionally we laughed and smiled just a little too.

Despite my initial reluctance to do any sort of group talk therapy, I began to look forward to those sessions more than I ever would have anticipated. None of us could entirely relate to the other's plight, but we shared our individual grief in a way that helped us leave each session with a sense that someone else just ... kind of understood. During a time when everything was new and unfamiliar and unwelcome and unpleasant and unhappy, it was comforting to feel that we could be ourselves, that no one would judge our emotions or our complaints. We didn't have to be any certain way for anyone else. We just got to be ourselves, and it was reassuring to know that someone else sort of "got it."

Those sessions taught me that sharing and venting and listening is *not* wallowing in negativity. It is not simply acquiescing and giving in to complaining and allowing our frustrations to take over. Rather, these kinds of sessions, formally structured or not, represent active participation in others' lives, and active participation in such a group session, with its emotion and pain, can be very positive. It can provide a much-needed outlet for healing. Sharing stress and suffering with others in a supportive setting can be very therapeutic and can assist in recovery. Every participant has the ability to provide invaluable moral support to others while simultaneously navigating his or her own individual path.

Thank you, Heidi. You inspired me in 1999 and your book *Fancy Feet* is a poignant read. I am ever so grateful that I shared a short, but meaningful, part of my early journey with you.

And thank you, Gail. I believe you occasionally look down on Heidi and me with your gleaming white teeth and your enthusiastic, encouraging smile. You were such a positive presence, a ray of light in a dark time. I'm so very sorry your time here was unfairly cut short.

Driving Forward

While I was earning my master's degree, I was fortunate to be given a paying teaching assistant position for undergraduate kinesiology students. I spent a great deal of time in the laboratory, and although I was an instructor, it was a tremendous learning opportunity for me too. The University of Ottawa had a medical school, and therefore we had access to specimens that were not available to me as an undergrad student at Brock University.

When I was shot, the knowledge that I gained by working in that lab became extremely helpful. That clinical knowledge, combined with the body awareness I had developed as a figure skater, assisted me tremendously with my amputee rehabilitation.

Not only was I better equipped to comprehend the physiology behind the medical issues I was facing, but I had unknowingly developed excellent proprioception. Essentially, proprioception is the awareness of where your body is in space, and this skill, while not one that had been deliberately taught, but rather a critical bonus, has assisted me greatly. In the early days, I would close my eyes, and at my physiotherapist's request, try to touch my rubberized right toes. I would reach down, confident I could easily find the place in space where my toes had always been, only to open my eyes and find out I was way off, six or eight inches off! It was infuriating to fail.

As an amputee, knowing where your foot is in space is imperative for walking success, and that was certainly my primary focus. However, during those monotonous months of daily rehab, there were other matters to attend to as well. For example, how would I deal with learning how to drive now that my right foot was no longer there?

In the early months, I was sent to a driver rehabilitation facility where they would test my physical abilities. I was barely used to my new prosthetic foot and was still using crutches and canes, but the requirement at the driver rehab facility was to quickly shift my foot onto a pedal as soon as an audible signal was received. The process was similar to that of a hearing test—press the button when you hear a sound. At driver training, those reaction time movements would be timed, and my results would determine the level of reaction time I (or more specifically, my leg) possessed. But it wasn't just the reaction time: the movement had to be accurate in landing in a certain position on the pedal. If I didn't reach the test standard, my driving privileges would not be reinstated.

So I sat there nervously awaiting the signal. Each time I heard it, I would awkwardly and hastily try to raise my leg and place my prosthetic foot on the pedal. Sometimes my foot made it—sort of—and sometimes my toe would touch the pedal and be positioned so that I could depress it. If that occurred, it would be loosely considered a win. I say "loosely" because if my toe ended up there, it was most likely a fluke.

The truth was, try as I might, I just couldn't figure out where my artificial foot was in space. Sometimes my heel would make contact with the pedal, but the toe would be positioned off to the side. That was not a win, despite my protests that my foot was technically on the pedal and able to depress it. Sometimes, my foot would miss the pedal entirely. I just had no awareness of where my body parts were anymore.

With each try I was increasingly frustrated and, frankly, I found it to be extremely embarrassing. A slow, panicky feeling began to simmer in my stomach. My results got worse.

OMG! What if I could never drive again?!

The next time I heard the signal, I looked down at my foot and silently willed it to move, believing that if I looked at it sternly, it would respond. But when I did move it, instead of being a precise and sharp and quick motion, it was slow and cumbersome and mostly inaccurate.

Not surprisingly, I flunked the reaction time test. I was told that driving with my prosthetic would *not* be an option.

I was simultaneously discouraged and livid. How dare they fail me? Didn't they know who I was, what I had been through? It was still early in my recovery. Didn't those things count for something? What would I do if I couldn't drive? How could I be an independent adult, let alone a police officer?

However, as time wore on and I became more accustomed to my leg, my steps and foot placement became more deliberate and precise. Control over my body was slowly improving, and I could now close my eyes, reach down with my hand, and touch my prosthetic toes—a monumental task for an amputee relearning spatial awareness.

I wanted to tackle that reaction time test again now that my proprioception, my awareness of where my body was in space, had vastly improved. Nervous, but humble, I returned to the driver assessment centre. The signal sounded, and I effortlessly and fluidly moved my leg onto the pedal. Over and over I did it, and did it well. I passed!

But that was only step #1.

I still had to retake my actual driver's test because, for me to drive legally, my licence now needed to indicate a provincially imposed restriction code on the back.

I returned to Kitimat and practised driving in my trusty 1989 Chrysler Dynasty. (I'm sure I was the only person under the age of sixty who drove one of those velour-interior beauties!) I drove around and around the town limits, practising every manoeuvre I could imagine. I brushed up on my shoulder checks, and steering wheel hand positions, and reviewed the rules and routines we learn as new, sixteen-year-old drivers.

At long last it was exam day, and I hopped into the vehicle with the driver examiner. I drove nervously around Kitimat trying to feign disinterest when local acquaintances I had not seen in months excitedly waved at me when they saw me behind the wheel. I was death-gripping my steering wheel at 10 and 2 o'clock, my eyes fixed on the road in front of me. I couldn't risk the distraction of acknowledging the passersby.

I flawlessly executed my test and I *passed*! I was more excited then, at twenty-nine, than I had been at sixteen! My licence was reinstated, the back bearing code #25—fitted prosthesis/leg brace required. Take that, for saying I couldn't drive with a prosthetic! I can! I still do!

But now I needed to prove to myself that I would be okay with hearing gunshots go off, and that meant that it was time to head to the firing range.

It required some psychological coaxing and a great deal of mental prep and rehearsal before I tackled it. The sounds, the smells—I knew they would bring the memories flooding back. I gathered my gun and drove slowly to the outdoor shooting range in Kitimat, mentally rehearsing tactics. When I arrived, I got out and looked around, taking time to absorb the surroundings, to think about how much this experience would tell me about my future, what I might not be able to handle. I closed my eyes and took long, deep breaths, willing myself to be strong.

After several minutes, I was ready. I got into position. I drew my pistol from the holster. I held it up, right eye closed, as I had so many times before. I aimed at the target, and I braced myself for the sound, the inevitable kickback of the gun. I breathed in, I fired, I breathed out. I slowly lowered my gun, taking it all in. And I realized I was … fine. Mostly. Maybe it was because the sound of the pistol is much different from the sound of a bullet from a sawed-off .303 rifle barrelling through my shin. I don't know exactly; I just know I was proud, very proud. Tears welled up in my eyes. Some trickled down my face. I had faced a huge fear, one that had been hanging over me for months, and I had overcome it.

I flew back to Vancouver, but I knew it was time to bring my Dynasty from Kitimat down to Vancouver so I could drive myself around and regain some independence. No more relying on taxis or other people, and a much-appreciated loaner car from a generous Vancouver dealership! I was excited, *not* to be driving my old Dynasty, but because of the freedom I would have now that my licence was reinstated. I arranged for a friend to ship my car to Vancouver, and on a whim, I asked that my mountain bike be sent along as well. It would be exhilarating to learn to ride it again and to cycle around the False Creek sea wall, I thought.

One evening shortly after my vehicle and bicycle arrived in Vancouver, symbolizing yet another step towards independence, I returned to my condo. As soon as I opened the door, I knew something was wrong. I thought I heard a noise upstairs and my senses were instantly heightened. I noticed some items on the main floor were slightly askew, definitely not how I had left them. That's when I realized my rental apartment had been broken into! Shaking, and terrified that the thieves might still be inside my unit, I hurried to a neighbour's and called the police.

When the police arrived and cleared the condo, deeming it safe, we did a walk-through together. My heart was still racing, and I was devastated to see that my condo was an absolute mess. The laptop I had been loaned from the RCMP was gone. My new Walkman, gifted to me by Sony, was gone. Dozens of CDs I used in that Walkman were gone. Learning to walk wouldn't be the same without those luxuries.

The mountain bike that I had been so excited to learn to use again? Gone. Most disconcerting of all was the fact that my drawers had been emptied onto the floor, and my underwear was strewn about everywhere. I was grossed out, devastated, traumatized.

The police officer investigating suggested that the thieves had entered via a patio door, but given the layout of the condo and the height of the patio doors, I felt that would have required Superman powers. Plus, I knew that that patio door had been locked when I left, and it was still locked. I believed that they had entered via a window on a landing right outside my bedroom on the second floor. A planter outside that window was askew, and my nightlight in the outlet indoors just below the window was slightly pulled out from the wall. I also saw a scuff mark, presumably from the sole of a shoe, on that wall close to the nightlight. I believed it was the entry point, and that entry point happened to be right beside my bedroom. All I could think of was the vulnerability I felt, knowing that a criminal had entered my temporary home, my supposed safe haven. That entry had taken place mere feet from where I slept every night, with my prosthetic leg off, alone in my condo.

I knew I couldn't stay there another moment.

I packed some belongings, loaded up my vehicle, and, with tears streaming down my face, drove around aimlessly. My mom had moved back to Brockville, and I had no local friends, so I had no one to call. I was extremely emotional and couldn't escape the terrifying and overwhelming feelings of helplessness, of being violated yet again. The prospect of being in that condo alone terrified me.

I drove to a hotel downtown, but there was no availability. Exhausted, I checked into a cheap motel across the street instead. Upon check-in there, staff advised me not to leave my belongings in my vehicle as there was no security (read: there *were* vandalism and thefts), so I got a luggage cart and loaded everything up. I entered my assigned room but was horrified at the state of it. It was disgusting, and I couldn't bring myself to sit on the bed-spread, let alone picture myself getting any rest in that bed. The sink and tub and toilet were lavender-coloured porcelain, but the insides were rimmed in brown. The toilet water was also a disgusting brownish grey. Bawling, I took a large gulp of Bailey's from the bottle in my baggage, looked at myself in the warped mirror in the dim light in the bathroom, took a breath and headed back to the check-in desk in the lobby, pushing my luggage cart. There was a lineup of what appeared to be ladies of the night and cheezy-looking johns booking in for short-term/hourly-rate visits. When it was my turn to speak to the staff at the front desk, I explained that the room was unacceptable, and I wanted a refund. The desk clerk was dismissive and refused the refund, but I was determined. I looked side to side and behind me at the lineup of guests, leaned forward, and quietly informed him that the room had bugs. His eyes got wide. He quickly shushed me so that other guests wouldn't overhear my complaint. He hastily processed a full refund, and I loaded up my vehicle for the second time that night. As I drove away, I admitted to myself that the fabrication about the bugs was not one of my finer moments, but after the stress of the break-in, and the truly disgusting state of the room, in that moment, I felt completely and utterly justified.

I found myself in Richmond, in a clean and safe hotel, and checked in for a sleepless night spent strategizing about how I could get out of the city for good.

The F#@*ing P.A.R.E.

From the beginning of my rehabilitation, I had been told that to be allowed to return to general policing duties, I must pass the dreaded P.A.R.E., the Physical Abilities Requirement Evaluation. The P.A.R.E. is used to assess a person's physical fitness and suitability for police work. This physical challenge now represented the one obstacle standing in the way of my resuming my life and reclaiming everything that had been so suddenly and wrongfully taken from me.

My first experience with the P.A.R.E. had taken place when I was an RCMP applicant. I had travelled from Brockville to Toronto to complete it as part of the application process. Since I was an aerobics instructor at the time, I had absolutely no concerns about being able to perform fitness tests. However, I had realized that day as I was struggling to regain my breath after running the course that, although I was aerobically fit, this test has a significant anaerobic component as well. Short bursts of intensity were not my strong point, and it took hours that day for my chest to stop heaving with every short, painful inhale.

Once at Depot, Lorelei and I had sweated and stressed over this P.A.R.E. for the duration of police training; to us it was a test to be loathed, feared, especially, it seemed, for females. One misstep, one off-day on test day, could jeopardize the entire six-month training process.

The news now that I *must* pass the P.A.R.E. to return to duty infuriated me because I had *never* heard of anyone being required to do this. I had never heard of it then, nor have I heard of it since. The idea of having this imposed on me angered me for several reasons. I have seen overweight members who are not able to climb a flight of stairs without being winded … yet they are deemed to be suitable for general duty policing. I have seen out-of-shape female members return from maternity leave and be deemed suitable for general duty policing. I have seen members come back to work after various injuries and still be deemed suitable for general duties. Etc.

All I could think was, "Why are the rules different for me?"

In my imagination, frustrated and bitter at the time, the only conclusion I could draw was that there was some conspiracy, some expectation that I would fail. I believed that if enough roadblocks were set up, I would inevitably fail and never be allowed to return to duty. It felt like management *wanted* me to fail.

My recovery progress seemed ridiculously slow, and I shed many, many tears during those months. I was emotional. Pain was unrelenting. My grief was palpable, my sorrow unbearable. Frustration was incessant. Loneliness was overwhelming.

To make things worse, because my wounds were slow to heal, obtaining a prosthetic leg was delayed, over and over. Each time I had an appointment to begin the fitting process, I would become excited and enter the doctor's office full of hope and optimism. The doctor would look at my scars, my stitches, Staub, and then deliver the news that, once again, I was not yet ready to start. I would require debriding, or more antibiotics, or more rest. I was so demoralized because of these delays. It was always *more time*, and each setback was another massive letdown. I was testy, irritable, and depressed. I wondered if anything would ever change.

Not only were there numerous delays, but each one seemed like an eternity in and of itself. I didn't cope well with that because I wanted desperately to get on with my life, and I was tired of waiting. Following each disappointment, I would reluctantly return to physio and bitterly continue to work on yet more range-of-motion exercises. I would stretch and I would halfheartedly exercise my upper body. I would watch with envy the amputees who already had their prosthetic legs and who were on their way out of physio, close to moving on, close to resuming their lives. Much of the time I was miserable, often an epic bitch.

But I persevered. Granted, I persevered because I had no alternative. But I persevered also because sometimes when something you have is taken away from you, deep down you desperately want to reclaim what is "rightfully" yours. You simply don't know how important some things are until you no longer have them.

One day, even before I was weight-bearing on my prosthetic leg and still relied entirely on two crutches, I crutched 20+ blocks home from physio, just to prove to myself I was capable. My independence had been taken from me, and sometimes I needed to do things that reminded me that I was in fact regaining some of the things that had been missing for so long. Progress was so gradual that occasionally I needed a little reminder that I was actually moving forward in measurable, appreciable ways.

Then one day—finally—it was time. Ricky, my prosthetist, fitted me for a socket, the most critical part of my prosthetic leg. Staub was covered with a light piece of fabric. Reference points were carefully drawn on the fabric with a sharpie. Those marks indicated the necessary landmarks for a good fit—pressure points, trouble areas, bony protrusions. Then, a wet, soggy, thick gauze-like material, the same as is used in emergency room casts for setting broken bones, was wrapped around my stump, over top of the thin marked-up fabric. The outer covering was skillfully, deliberately, and continuously smoothed over by my prosthetist for several minutes, slowly drying and hardening into a more permanent representation of the shape of my stump. Just when it was almost fully dried, yet slightly malleable, Ricky carefully and expertly pulled it off my stump. The marks from the sharpie had transferred onto the inside of the cast mould, indicating key areas of my leg that were likely to require closer attention during the next phase of fitting. I left his office that day wondering what the next step would be, eager to move forward, yet anxious about what lay ahead.

I returned to Ricky a few days later to be presented with a clear plastic "check" socket, a practice socket of sorts. It was a see-through mould of my stump attached to a pole. That pole, complete with visible bolts and screws, had a human sized, Barbie-type replica of a foot attached to the bottom, although in actuality it was a size 10 woman's foot. I put it on and stared in disbelief—oh, to see my body with *two* feet again! To see *two* shoes instead of a single left shoe underneath me was glorious!

It also seemed like a creation made from the hardware section of Home Depot! And I soon realized that the entire fitting process would take place in a room resembling a car mechanic's garage. The whole prosthetist's office was more like a maintenance workshop than a medical clinic, and the sterile laboratory-like process I had envisioned was certainly not reality.

The following days were filled with more fittings, repeat visits to Ricky, and a whole bunch of sensory overload. Staub was still swollen, and the scars were torturous reminders of what I had been through. I was only allowed to try on my leg and wear it for short periods before I had to relinquish it again. I wasn't allowed to take it home with me overnight, as Linda, my physiotherapist, had figured out that I was stubborn and couldn't be trusted not to wear it longer than instructed. It was tempting to try it and push through the pain in hopes of regaining my independence more quickly, but my wise physiotherapist and my expert prosthetist had anticipated that keenness—it was why they took my leg away from me! I just couldn't see that wearing my new leg was a huge physical adjustment and a process that could *only* be undertaken while being closely supervised and monitored. The whole situation was laborious and time-consuming and painful. It was stressful and frustrating when my stump wouldn't accept more pressure, and I would easily become exhausted simply from wearing it. Too much pressure, prolonged or too direct, would cause sores on my thin, damaged, recently stitched skin. Direct pressure on other areas would cause blisters that seemed to take forever to heal.

Slowly, ever so slowly, modifications were made to the shape of the socket. The alignment of the pole and foot was carefully adjusted for my height, for how my weight is distributed, and for how I walk. It is a tricky process, a science guided largely by my feedback, and takes place under the watchful eyes of well-trained professionals.

As time wore on, I was able to bear weight for gradually increasing periods of time. Each milestone was exhilarating, but I had to truly learn to listen to my body; ignoring signals equalled sores, and even the most minor sores could set me back for days, even weeks.

Then one day, I was scheduled to be a guest on a Vancouver television talk show. Since my shooting had generated a great deal of media coverage, I had already done several interviews and I wasn't nervous. I went to physio in the morning and went through my regular rehab routine, expecting this day to be no different than the ones preceding it. I donned my leg, went through my supervised routine, and then went to remove my prosthetic to hand it back to my Linda, just as I always did. After all, I had never been allowed to take my prosthetic leg out of the rehab facility, let alone keep it for a sleepover!

When I was packing up my backpack readying to leave rehab, however, Linda looked me in the eyes and said with a twinkle in her eye, "You can take it with you." Finally! This was the news I had been anxiously awaiting. I was given the green light to take, and wear, my leg *outside* the facility! Excitedly, I departed that day, honoured to be wearing my leg, and more than ready to show it off to the world! I arrived at the set of the TV show, triumphant and hardly able to contain myself. I was so ridiculously proud of my new gear; it seemed like such an accomplishment. I simply couldn't stop grinning, beaming while having my TV makeup applied!

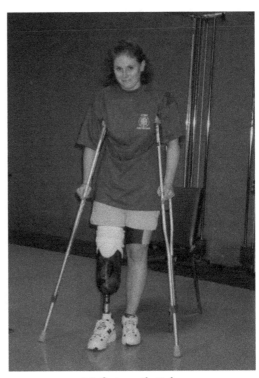

My first prosthetic leg.

I collapsed into my bed that night, drained from all the excitement and utterly exhausted from the physical strain of wearing my leg for longer than I ever had. While I had to promise to adhere to the strict directions about how much time to spend with it on, I had gotten to wear it! The world began to open up in many new and exciting ways!

Under close supervision, I slowly, and painstakingly, relearned how to stand.

I learned how to balance on two feet again. After months of using only one foot as a base of support, my centre of gravity had shifted so much that I didn't know how to stand upright on two feet anymore. Linda would make me close my eyes and place each foot on a scale. With her there to catch me should I topple, I would position my body where I felt that my body weight would be evenly distributed on each scale. When I was confident I was 50/50 and that my weight was equally shared between the scales, I would apprehensively open my eyes, look down, and realize that, in fact, 90 percent of my weight was on my (good) left leg, while only 10 percent was on my right. It took months to build confidence in my prosthetic equipment, to use the equipment as intended, and to test its limitations to prove to myself that it could be trusted to hold me up. Mostly I had to learn to trust myself and retrain my muscles to stabilize my body in its new state. Since I have no foot or ankle, other joints and muscles must step up to compensate. The process of regaining my independence was lengthy; my body had failed me over and over, so rebuilding faith in its new and different capabilities was difficult.

Learning to walk again.

I gradually learned to walk and would constantly catch myself looking at reflections in windows to satisfy myself that I wasn't limping. I had no tolerance for anything less than a perfect gait.

I never took a break because I recognized early on that having a routine was critical, even if progress was snail-like. I was tenacious and relentless, and I knew that my whole life revolved around the routine I had established. Get up. Shower. Eat breakfast. Get to physio first thing in the morning, chauffeured there by my mother or by one of my regular taxi drivers. I would stay until lunch time, then hit the neighbourhood gym hard in the afternoon, trying to forget the fact that I was surrounded by dozens of young, able-bodied, hip, urban, beautiful model-type Vancouverites. (I called that gym "the land of the beautiful people.") I would take long walks in the evening, concentrating on gait and calculated, repetitive foot placement. I wanted walking to become natural again. I wanted it to feel ... normal. Then I would try to get some sleep. And I would repeat it all the next day.

Linda and I hiked in Queen Elizabeth Park, climbing rock walls, manoeuvring in the gardens, climbing small trees. We walked up and down hills—pavement, gravel, sand—to ensure I was developing balance. We went to skating rinks and swimming pools to determine what challenges those environments and activities would present. I practised kicking and punching.

Learning to trust my equipment.

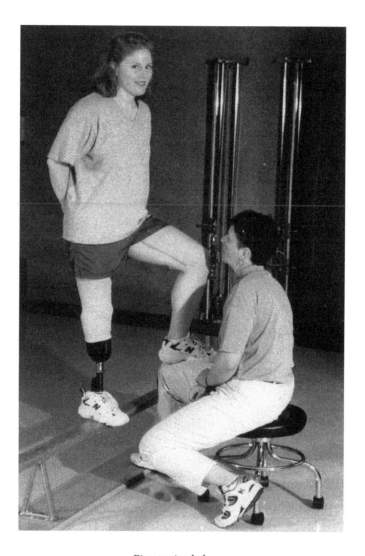

Fine-tuning balance.

I stood on rocks and benches and curbs and foam and BOSU balls to challenge my confidence.

I cycled, and occasionally Linda made me deliberately fall off so she could be confident that I would in fact be able to get back up, if it happened in an unsupervised setting.

Linda simulated emergency situations by making up scenarios based on possible real-life emergencies. She would darken the room. I would lie down with my leg off, like I would be if I were sleeping. She would pretend there was a fire alarm. I would have to feel around for my leg equipment, put it on, step into my prosthetic leg socket, secure it, and escape the "fire." We practised where I would leave my leg at night, where my equipment would be best positioned so it could be easily and quickly located and put on at a moment's notice. Those exercises assisted in alleviating my feelings of vulnerability and helped restore my confidence in being able to handle an emergency.

I was fitted for a high heel leg and pranced around on it with high heel boots. After months of wearing only sneakers and exercise clothes, it was thrilling to feel *female* again! It seemed like the instant I put those boots on, my posture immediately improved; it was pride and newfound poise, simply a result of my footwear!

I felt the freedom of once again participating in the things I loved, and I even slowly, slowly learned to run. Even for a non-runner, simply being able to move like that again was an indescribably incredible feeling. The fact that I could actually do it again helped make me forget that I had always hated running! We put tape on the walls and floors of the rehab facility hallways to indicate start and finish lines, and I sprinted back and forth, while Linda timed me. Tracking my improving speed was much-needed evidence to show progress; after all, I had just had months of what seemed to me to be no progress at all.

Learning to run.

Learning to rollerblade.

I relearned how to rollerblade.

And ice skate.

Each activity or sport required specific equipment, modifications, and practice, but I was determined to be as successful as I could possibly be, and Ricky was more than willing to ensure that happened. Ricky's passion to see me progress and excel, his unparalleled, intuitive ability to just "know" what I need, and his skill in providing me the right equipment have always been impressive (and for those reasons, no matter my geographical location, I *always* come back to him, his expertise, and his team).

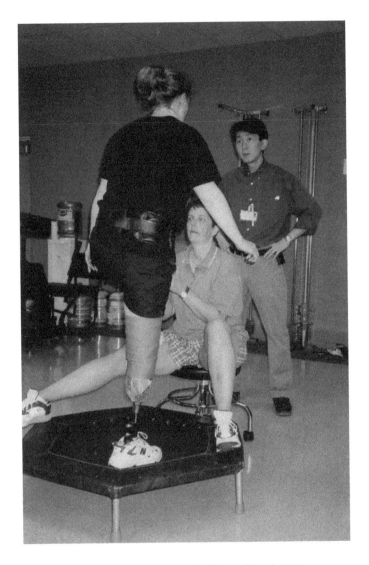

Learning from the experts – Ricky Chu and Linda McLaren.

So with Ricky and Linda's support, I slowly started to take pride in my accomplishments, accomplishments that, just months before, would never even have been considered an accomplishment at all. Walking, ascending and descending stairs, riding escalators, running, skating—they were all things I had long taken for granted.

I was so driven, so motivated, that my family and my medical team had to trick me into taking a break. Around Easter, Linda, much to my chagrin, delivered the news that *she* was going to take some time off. I thought, "How could she?!" I have so much to do and I *can't* do it without her! Annoyed, I allowed her to convince me to take a break for the same few days; after all, she wouldn't be there anyway. Reluctantly, I took a short reprieve, only to learn months later that the whole thing had been orchestrated to force *me* to take a much-needed break. She had never actually taken that time off at all!

Because of ongoing changes in my residual limb (my stump), including swelling reduction and muscle atrophy, it was an ever-changing shape. As an amputee, until there is some stability in stump size, it is extremely challenging to obtain a well-fitting prosthesis. In June 1999, I had an ill-fitting prosthetic, but I was hell-bent on completing the P.A.R.E. and getting out of Vancouver. It was time; I was done with the monotonous routine that I had been keeping for too many months. I was lonely and desperate to move on. Plus, I had convinced myself that determination, perseverance, and sheer willpower would and could only yield success. It was simply mind over matter, and I felt I was more than ready to make it happen.

So, one day in June, anxious to reclaim my life and depart Vancouver for good, I attended the RCMP "E" Division headquarters gym with my two biggest supporters—my mom and Linda. My goal was to complete the P.A.R.E. test; I just *had* to, because my future depended on it.

I stretched and warmed up and then nervously signalled to Mom and Linda when I was finally ready to begin.

On your mark, get set, GO! I lumbered through the first few laps, floundering step by step to get through the various obstacles. I was not graceful or agile; rather, I was awkward and heavy. My leg was cumbersome. I huffed and I puffed, and my leg hurt.

As I rounded the fourth lap, in pain and quite obviously struggling with each step, I focused on the next obstacle. It was the easiest one—a simple knee-high jump. It consisted solely of a thin wooden stick propped up by two low orange pylons. Simple, or so it should be. I plodded towards it, and time seemed to stand still. I "jumped" gracelessly into the air. The gymnasium was silent. My prosthesis did not clear the pole. I tripped. The wooden stick between the pylons came crashing down loudly on the gym floor, and the sound of it bouncing on the varnished hardwood floor echoed in the silent gym, taunting me. I fell in a crumpled heap to the ground, exhausted, sore, and utterly furious. The silence was deafening.

I burst into tears. I sobbed loudly. Mom and Linda couldn't find words, but their facial expressions said it all. They were as heartbroken as I. I cursed. A lot. I "fucked" and "holy fucked" and used every other curse word in my repertoire, and I uttered them all vehemently many, many times. The wooden stick was the enemy, as was my prosthetic leg; both had failed me. I angrily fired them both across the floor and vowed that I would never, ever put myself through such an impossible experience again. All my hard work had *not* paid off. I was obviously incapable, and I would give up on this godforsaken P.A.R.E. because, clearly, giving up was the only logical conclusion.

I departed the gym that day with no intention of ever returning. It was long past time to find a new direction, a new focus, one that did not revolve around obsessing about the P.A.R.E. or resuming police work. That point had been made painfully obvious to me and to my mom and to Linda that day.

So, for the next several days, Linda and I spent many hours talking about the future, what-iffing about next steps, my physical capabilities, my limitations. Slowly, and without me even really knowing it, she gradually reopened my mind to possibility. As we continued to talk, we began to identify some realistic expectations. My mind began to shift slightly, and I started to come around to the idea that maybe I wasn't really, truly ready to concede defeat.

Then, in July, merely six weeks later, with a better-fitting leg, a newfound and deep-rooted commitment to *not* allow myself to be a quitter, I apprehensively re-entered that same gymnasium with only Linda by my side. The building was old, and the familiar smells of the wood, the varnish, and the sweat filled my nostrils. I was overcome with fear and trepidation simply being there, but this day, we had told ourselves, *it would just be a practice.* We needed to train on the actual P.A.R.E. course because obstacles were so specific and difficult to replicate in the physio environment. Linda was going to videotape me so we could analyze the footage afterwards and determine where we could improve my technique, where we could shave off time so that I might in fact be successful at some point down the road.

I warmed up, loosened my muscles, and looked around the gym, taking it all in.

Here is the play-by-play:

Linda prepares the video camera. She gives me the start signal and I begin to run.

> Lap 1 – Feels pretty good …

> Lap 2 – I'm warmed up, new leg is staying on well. I'm pleasantly surprised …

> Lap 3 – Methodically and purposefully, I round the corners of the course and navigate the obstacles.

> Lap 4 – I'm getting tired but still have more energy than I expected. Oddly, I'm getting some renewed motivation. The memory of my previous fall on this very lap is hitting me hard. I'm worried. Will I fall again?

> Lap 5 – Geez, pretty good. Up and down, on and off the floor for the obstacles, almost there.

> Lap 6 – The final lap. *Holy shit.* I'm almost there! Sweating and breathing heavily, I round the last corner of the sixth lap. I remain focused and take each step, one at a time, carefully placing my sneaker and watching my footing. I'm totally focused on my right foot and where it is landing.

> Six laps completed. I am physically tired but I'm also feeling excited as it dawns on me. Success! I've completed all the laps! And I've done them pretty darned well!

I take a big breath and head quickly to the push/pull station. I grab the handle and push forward, leaning in, balancing on my toes, moving my feet around the machine in a semi-circle. I let go and pull the handles back, leaning my body weight backwards. I plant my feet confidently, dig in with my heels, and again move my feet deliberately in a half-circle around the machine. My prosthetic positioning is excellent, very stable. All in all, easy. As it turns out, all that upper body range of motion and weight training in the boring, early, non-leg-wearing days really did help!

Finally, I head to the heavy bag. I pick it up forcefully, sling it over my shoulder and proceed to carry it for the required distance. I drop it to the floor and wipe the sweat off my nose with my T-shirt.

Huffing and puffing, red-faced from the exertion, I look over at Linda, and reality slowly sinks in. I realize I have done it. I have conquered it. It dawns on me that that *might* just be it. Linda had videotaped that run for educational purposes, but could the past few minutes of my life really represent The End of the F#@*ing P.A.R.E.? Could we present that as evidence proving my abilities? Could it actually and finally be time to move on?

But I couldn't celebrate. It was too premature, too dangerous. I had to be cautious. After months and months of delays, letdowns, disappointments, frustrations, setbacks, failures, I couldn't let my emotions and the excitement get ahead of me.

Linda submitted that videotape of me doing the P.A.R.E. to RCMP Health Services. They had to review it carefully because they held the ultimate decision-making authority. Things were uncomfortably and entirely out of my hands, but as the weeks wore on and reality sank in, I felt more and more pride because I knew in my heart that I could not have performed that test any better than I just had.

Jumping Through Hoops

It wasn't until weeks later, after a great deal of anxiety, wondering, self-reflection, and uncertainty, that I finally received the phone call I had long awaited. RCMP Health Services was on the other end of the phone, and I was, at long last, given the green light to return to duties. Upon hearing the news, I shrieked with delight! I was beyond thrilled to learn that I was done with that godforsaken P.A.R.E. test. To me, it had been the only thing preventing me from resuming my life.

But my excitement was short-lived.

I was hastily preparing to leave Vancouver for good when, much to my dismay, the news arrived that the P.A.R.E. really wasn't the only test I was required to complete. I was now being told that I must meet several other standards before I could resume general policing duties.

I must do computerized use-of-force scenarios.

I must do police driving.

I must do firearms qualifications.

I must complete supervised ride-alongs.

I must receive approval from a psychologist.

There was suddenly *so* much left to do, and my reaction to this most unwelcome news was less than positive. Instantly I became angry—very, very angry. All my conspiracy theories came flooding back. Was the RCMP against me? Had they been expecting me to fail the P.A.R.E. and were now panicking about liability should I work again? Were they still hoping I failed at something by putting new obstacles in front of me, new hoops to jump through? By putting more in front of me, did they believe the odds of me not passing something would increase? Why would they do that? But what else could it be? I had spent months obsessing about the P.A.R.E. and, apparently against the odds, I had succeeded. Why now would there be other hurdles abruptly and inconsiderately thrown in my direction?

I was furious and extremely frustrated, and I only very, very slowly simmered down, due in large part to a harsh email I received from Linda. That very direct email contained many unpleasant, but truthful, comments about my bad attitude. However, her final point was most powerful. It reads:

> *"Do something with your fuse. It's pretty obvious it's short on this issue, and that in itself says something."*

By this time, Linda and I had spent countless hours together, and I had an incredible amount of respect for her. She was insightful and always posed thought-provoking questions. She expertly analyzed my physical capabilities—muscles, flexibility, range of motion, posture, weight-bearing habits—and ensured I improved them all. She was compassionate and able to read my emotions with an unparalleled degree of intuition and sensitivity. She pushed me to my full abilities, yet understood when to back off. My moodiness tested her patience frequently, but her persistence and support, along with her unwavering commitment to seeing me reach my goals, allowed me to exceed even my own expectations. Linda was so many things to me: teacher, coach, motivator, confidante, trainer, mentor, counsellor, massage therapist—and an expert physiotherapist! Most importantly, the bond we built in 1999 remains strong, and she continues to be a cherished friend.

So when I received that email from her, I was embarrassed. I was being petty and immature. I needed to be chastised. I deserved to be put in my place. *She* was exactly the one to do it.

As I slowly processed these new requirements, I had a few sporadic, more rational moments. I began to realize that, when I put it into perspective, none of these other obstacles would be as challenging as the F#@*ing P.A.R.E. The newly imposed requirements were all enormous nuisances and checking each thing off my now-revised to-do list would take more time, time that I was very unhappy to have to spend. But as I had been doing with every obstacle thrown my way in the preceding months, I broke things down and pieced things off into manageable steps.

I quickly made an appointment with a certified instructor to complete the scenario-based interactive use-of-force (FATS) simulations. I had to demonstrate that I was capable of reasonable, justifiable, in-the-moment decision-making.

Nervously I stood in the darkened room, equipped with my gun belt, facing the massive computer screen. The scenario began to unfold, and I went into work mode. Although interacting with a computer screen is much different from interacting with live human beings and real physical environments, I became caught up in my actor role. I communicated with the characters on the screen calmly, rationally, loudly, or authoritatively, depending on the scenario playing out on the screen. When the lights in the darkened room came back on, I turned anxiously to the instructor to hear my results. Pass! I had successfully completed my scenarios. I had proven to the instructor, and by extension the RCMP, that I was capable of appropriately using our various force options.

Whew.

Unexpected post-P.A.R.E. hoop #1—check!

Next, I was required to redo my police driving certifications, ensuring I could safely navigate the driving track within a certain designated time frame.

Full of performance anxiety, I attended the track. I was intimidated because track driving is not exactly the same as retaking a basic driver's test in a 1989 Chrysler Dynasty! Fortunately, the driving instructor assigned to me was very supportive, and with his encouragement, I successfully completed the course. In fact, I completed it three times in three different types of vehicles (an SUV, a standard police cruiser, and a Mustang)! My passing report states, "Her skills are above average." It was an absolute adrenaline rush to bask in the revelation that just months before, I'd had no idea if I would ever be allowed, or physically able, to drive. Now, I could drive, and I could drive fast! And safely! It was exhilarating! I was in control again! I was confident, capable, independent.

Hoop #2—check!

I was required to go to a shooting range to do my firearms qualifications. I needed to prove to the RCMP that not only could I still shoot well but that I wouldn't falter psychologically or seize up if I found myself in a real-life situation where it was necessary to draw my weapon.

I went to the range and I sailed through my target shooting qualifications, even exceeding the "Sharpshooter" designation: Pistol Course of Fire 234/250 and Shotgun Course of Fire 45/45! The report states, "She was eager to learn," "Excellent outlook and positive attitude," "Performed all aspects in a superior fashion." *BAM!*

Hoop #3—check!

Next, the RCMP had decided that I was required to do a couple of ride-alongs with a regular member. I would accompany that member on patrol and function like I did when I was a brand new constable on probation in 1996.

The thought of doing these was embarrassing as I felt like I was going to work, only to be babysat by a peer. To minimize the humiliation, I orchestrated the ride-alongs so that I could do them with Lorelei, who was now posted to Kelowna. That allowed us a social visit, as I would stay with her in her home, but it also provided me the opportunity to reintegrate myself into the policing world slowly while surrounded by a supportive friend and her colleagues.

Despite some moments of hesitation and adjusting to carrying out my policing duties with a prosthetic leg, it was so exciting to be back out there in the field in uniform! So much hinged on me performing well, however, and I took those shifts very seriously. On our last night shift, I was quickly reminded that some levity was necessary, fundamental in fact, for coping with the stress of the job. Lorelei and I pulled over a vehicle in a traffic stop, and as we approached the vehicle, we noticed some marijuana seeds in an open cardboard box in the rear seat. Lorelei looked at the driver, then looked at me with a smirk and stated to the driver, "You don't exactly strike me as the botanist type." I burst into laughter. The driver laughed nervously, although I am unclear as to whether he even knew what a botanist was! Either way, it was a well-timed and much-needed reminder that for months I had been so laser-focused on my rehabilitation, my performance, and subsequent successful completion of the return-to-work prerequisites, that I had lost sight of the importance of having a sense of humour. I had been too business-like, too un-fun. I had somehow grown to believe that allowing myself to enjoy life would indicate lack of commitment to rehab and compromise my focus. Laughter symbolized a release, and I had rarely been willing to engage in such a luxury; after all, I had serious goals to accomplish!

In the days that followed, I reflected on that moment a lot. I realized that although I had checked off most of the formal to-do list, it was time to relearn how to perform my duties in a way that worked for me. Since I have always been a firm believer that, as police officers, it is critical that we find some laughter in our day-to-day responsibilities, I knew that it was time to allow my personality to resurface. For me, having a sense of humour and finding bits of amusement are fundamental components of coping, of being truly successful, regardless of what I'm doing. My confidence had gradually improved, the ride-alongs had gone well, my mindset was shifting back into policing mode, and I was getting back in my groove. Even better … I was learning to *laugh* again!

Hoop #4—check!

Finally, though, I had to obtain psychological clearance.

Geesh! The truth was that I worried about this assessment more than the other requirements because I really had no idea what to expect. The injury and recovery had … changed me. They had changed my brain, and I was still figuring out my new normal. This assessment was *not* performance-based, and the subjective findings of a complete stranger were going to be entirely out of my control. I was terrified. What if I failed now? What if, after the gruelling months of recovery, this final hurdle prevented me from succeeding?

I sifted through the list of pre-approved health care providers and made an appointment with someone with an office close by. After all, the sooner I could knock this off my to-do list, the better. Apprehensively, I attended the office, anxious to get this step checked off. I *had* to leave with a signature that confirmed I was psychologically able to return to work. I *had* to have this much-needed approval.

A stuffy-looking older man wearing a suit and a stiff demeanour opened the door. With an accent I couldn't quite identify, he introduced himself, and I was instantly disheartened. What kind of connection and rapport would the two of us be able to establish for me to obtain the approval signatures I so desperately required?

All my fears were being realized. My whole future hung in the hands of a stranger from a completely different background. "He won't understand," I thought miserably. I would never be able to convey how much his assessment meant to me. What if he didn't think I was ready to return to work? What would I do then? What could I say to beg him, to convince him I was ready? Would someone with his experience and training and background be able to see right through me? After all, he was an expert. "I'm doomed," I admitted to myself with a heavy heart.

Minutes later, however, I realized that we could in fact talk easily. He was down-to-earth and understanding, and most importantly, he was supportive and encouraging. The conversation was effortless, and the seemingly apparent differences and barriers I had perceived at the outset of our meeting were no longer relevant. I had been naïve and judgmental in being so pessimistic.

We scheduled the rest of the required assessment appointments, and lo and behold, shortly thereafter, he provided a report to the RCMP. He gave me the green light to go back to work!

Hoop #5—check!

Then, finally then, I was done. I could go back to work. This time it was real. No more obstacles. None. I had nailed them all. *Every. Single. One.*

I was brimming with pride. For ten long months, I had been unrelenting, focused, driven. I had persevered and I had succeeded. I had overcome so much, both personally and professionally. Against so many odds, I had validated myself, to myself. That was the most meaningful part of the entire previous nine months. I proved to myself that I was capable.

But now what?

Accessorizing

I deserved a new vehicle. After everything I had been through, I simply couldn't continue driving a 1989 Chrysler Dynasty! I need something cooler, more symbolic of my success, more fun, more *me*.

I called up an old university friend and asked him to come with me to the Honda dealer. I knew I wanted a CR-V—I had been eyeing them up for ages—but my friend negotiates contracts for a living, and I knew he was the man to assist me in getting the best deal.

Excitedly (well, I, far more so than he), we entered the Honda showroom, and the salesman started rhyming off the standard information. Mileage, features, added options, pricing. Unable to focus on those details, I sat in the demo vehicle in the showroom and kept looking back and forth at my friend and then the salesman. I was too excited to participate in the discussion about the relevant matters. I couldn't focus. I mean, this *had* to be my new vehicle! Finally, they became silent, looking expectantly at me for a reasonably intelligent question, something about the fancy features the vehicle offered, or something about cost … but no. With a raised eyebrow and a sideways smirk, all I could muster up was, "Does this vehicle *work* for me? Like, if you pulled up beside me at a stoplight would you think I *suit* this vehicle?" Perplexed, they both looked at me. My friend was caught off-guard, but mildly amused. The salesman had most likely never been faced with such a moronic question. But to me, this was a big question. As silly as it may have been, I was resuming my life. I was proud of who I had become, what I had accomplished. My Chrysler Dynasty was reflective of the *old* me, the two-legged me who depended on my parents, who hadn't quite "arrived" as an adult. It was a part of my past, and this new vehicle had to represent my accomplishments since then, my future. I viewed it as a statement accessory, and I *love* accessories. I simply wanted to know if I wore that vehicle well.

I believed it did work for me, and I bought that vehicle. And I loved it, just as I knew I would. To me, that CR-V symbolized my hard work and my well-earned freedom. It stood for independence and adulthood, pride and perseverance. It was a reward, some light at the end of a long, dark, frightening tunnel.

Returning to Duty

I had long ago decided that should I ever be approved and able to return to general policing duties, I would do so in Kitimat, even though I knew that was an unpopular decision for some of my family members, friends, and even colleagues. Since my shooting had presented an opportunity to transfer out of Kitimat, many believed that I should move closer to family and return to Ontario. I knew, though, that if I transferred somewhere new, I would still be starting over—new town, new colleagues, new faces in the community, new neighbourhoods. Starting fresh in an unfamiliar community, not knowing local procedures or even just the layout of the streets, would add unnecessary complications to an already stressful return-to-work situation. It would be like starting from scratch, merely a few years after I had already boldly done that on my own. I had given the idea of moving again a great deal of thought, but had decided that I wanted and, more importantly, I *needed* to return to a place I knew. I didn't want to relocate; I just simply couldn't put myself through it again. I had moved to Kitimat, then unexpectedly had to move to Vancouver, and the idea of moving again was simply too much. I recognized that it was essential for me to have some familiarity after so much change, so much upheaval. I wanted to reduce my risk of failing, and I thought that if I could go where I knew policing, where I knew the layout of the town, where I knew my co-workers and many community members, my chances of successfully returning to work would be much higher. I had to minimize the impact of the day-to-day logistics. But on a deeper level, I was acutely aware that the most important goal in me returning to work was proving myself to *myself*.

I packed up my new, fancy, blue Honda; bought some uplifting, empowering music CDs to listen to en route to Kitimat; and set out to complete the final piece of regaining my life. I drove eight hours to Prince George, stayed overnight in a mediocre hotel, and then drove another eight hours to Kitimat, pep-talking the whole way. I sang Cher anthem songs over and over, personalizing the lyrics. I sang those words loudly. And they were accompanied by enthusiastic fist pumping, and driver's seat dance moves. I was excited. I knew in my heart that I had earned every single fist pump on that sixteen-hour trek.

On October 4, 1999, just ten months after losing my right leg in that fateful shooting, I returned to regular general patrol duties in Kitimat. I was exhilarated. I was nervous but so very ready. I couldn't wait for my first shift back and I proudly put my uniform on and awaited my first call.

Back to duty!

Finally, that long-anticipated dispatch call came.

I excitedly answered my portable radio, eager to race out to help, to serve my community. I was *baaaaack*! Instead, in true northern B.C. policing style, I was dispatched to a ... wait for it ... *bear* call! Yes, a bear call. Admittedly, it wasn't what I had hoped for, but I raced out of the detachment building like there was a B&E in progress! I drove around and eagerly conducted some very thorough bear patrols. As was often the case with these kinds of calls, I never did end up spotting that bear, but I maintain that they were the most enthusiastic bear patrols ever conducted by any police officer anywhere in the world!

More importantly, it is believed that that October day made me the first and only police officer in Canada with an artificial leg to have returned to full, unrestricted general policing duties.

Falling Down

When I returned to Kitimat, I desperately wanted all of my former life back. I gradually resumed my activities and tried to get back to where I had left off. That included synchronized skating on my adult precision team. My team was a group of former figure skaters who wanted to get back on the ice and feed our love for the sport. We would go out and practise for an hour a week, and I loved it!

Then, the annual figure skating club show approached. That show brought me back to a series of childhood stressors and a whole host of weird memories. Shows were our one chance every year to show our parents and our friends what we could do, except that usually what we did in the show was not actually performing our tricks and demonstrating our accomplishments. We were given roles that often required no skill at all. One year I dressed up as The Count from *Sesame Street*, complete with a giant head I could hardly see out of! Another year when I was assigned one of the coveted solo spots, one where I could wear a pretty dress, I was so anxious that I could hardly sleep in the days leading up to the show. Those nerves resulted in me falling in that solo while attempting to execute a simple axel, a trick I easily did dozens of times daily. That fall embarrassed me in front of my parents and a high school boyfriend, and I hustled off the ice to sit in shame in the dressing room. It took ages for me to gather the courage to face anyone, and for days I kicked myself for falling on such an easy move.

But this time, as an adult in 2000, I was part of a team, and we had never gotten to perform in front of an audience. The decision was made, we had a goal, and our team was added to the show program.

With my prosthetic leg, I could do *most of* the routine, and my teammates were patient. I was nervous, but the only move I really struggled with was a backwards-skating drag. I just couldn't get my prosthetic leg into that position, but it was nothing that a simple strategic cheat move couldn't cover up. Costumes had come a long way since my youth, and I was nervously excited to skate in front of the community members in attendance. The music began, and we pushed off. Around and around we went, and I craftily and carefully cheated my way through the annoyingly impossible back drag. Having that move out of the way brought a huge sigh of relief, and now the post-skating show celebratory cocktail hour was imminent! Then, on a simple Mohawk turn, a simple direction-changing move that I had learned as a child, I found myself sitting on my ass on the ice. To be clear, because of the momentum we had with our linked arms, I was sliding on my ass across the ice, sort of being pulled along by my supportive teammates who were trying not to fall down themselves. When the sliding stopped and I was able to get up and collect myself, I was humiliated. It felt exactly like when I had fallen doing my axel in that show so many years ago.

Yet this time, the humiliation was fleeting and the feelings that fall generated were vastly different. My take-aways, unlike years before when I had had performance anxiety, and far longer lasting embarrassment, were more profound. I had lost my leg and been fitted with a skating prosthetic. I had rejoined my team, my friends, my social circle. I had practised and belonged.

I had fallen, but this time, I laughed and awkwardly got back up. I wiped the snow off my dress and flashed a huge smile to the audience.

As I age, I know there will be many more falls, some more public than others. I don't want to hide in the dressing room, embarrassed to come out. I don't want to stew about such silly, meaningless things. Red-faced or not, I just want to keep laughing and smiling when I do eventually find my way back to my feet.

Recognition

When I successfully returned to work, I was *thrilled* to be back. Returning to work was something I did for myself; I had been consumed with reclaiming my life and regaining my independence, so that accomplishment was purely about personal goals.

Months later, in 2000, I received notification that a member of the public, a stranger to me, had nominated me for a highly prestigious award. As a result of her submission, I was to receive a Governor General's Meritorious Service Medal.

I was most honoured by the gesture, and the woman who had forwarded my name for consideration was so humble she didn't even want acknowledgement.

At the Governor General's ceremony, I met a variety of influential Canadian citizens from all walks of life. To my delight, I was in the company of champion figure skaters Shae-Lynn Bourne and Victor Kraatz! Each award presentation at that ceremony was preceded by a brief description of what the person had done that was so remarkable, so extraordinary, so worthy of recognition. With each summary, my amazement grew. I simply could not believe that *my name* was included with this calibre of people!

Shortly thereafter, I received notification that I would be receiving a Medal of Valour from the International Association of Women in Policing (IAWP), an association with which I had no affiliation. Again, I was humbled that my efforts in returning to work had been noticed and recognized.

At that ceremony, I found myself again in the company of true heroes, fellow police officers who had been involved in groundbreaking investigations, colleagues who had accomplished remarkable things, been in involved in incredible acts of bravery. Once more, I was honoured to be included in such a group.

A few years later I was inducted into my hometown high school's Hall of Fame, and I was pleased to be recognized so long after having left my hometown. I was flattered that my photo would be displayed in the hallway of the school that had helped form me, the school my brothers and I had all attended, the school where my parents and brothers and I had all spent so much time—learning, playing, teaching, and coaching.

In 2012, I was honoured that my former elementary school in my hometown dedicated their park to four local "heroes," one being me.

From the RCMP, I received a Commanding Officer's Commendation, and later, a Commanding Officer's Letter of Appreciation and a Queen's Diamond Jubilee medal.

I don't mention those awards to be boastful. Of course, I'm proud of them, but more importantly, I feel humbled and fortunate to have been honoured in public ways. However, every day tremendous work is being done by our RCMP members all around this country and abroad, and that work often goes unnoticed. I hear stories of heroism and bravery and I have personally witnessed these kinds of acts. I also know they happen everywhere. Police sometimes work alone and handle very complicated people. They courageously enter dangerous situations, putting their own safety in jeopardy for the greater good of the people they serve. They work in specialty units that require extensive training. They volunteer in their communities. Even off-duty members, without their issued equipment, are compelled to act to preserve public safety.

While some would argue that we "signed up to do this," and that anything we face in the course of our day-to-day duties is simply "part of the job," I firmly take a different stance. Does the fact that we are law enforcement officers make us different from anyone else? Teachers? Firefighters? Restaurant wait staff?

Many jobs can be somewhat thankless, but we don't shy away from giving our child's teacher a gift card at Christmas and at year end. We seem to universally revere all firefighters. We reward our wait staff with a customary tip, often even for mediocre service. But as police officers, did we simply relinquish all desire to be appreciated when we received our badge? Is selflessly serving others, on or off duty, and often 24/7, just considered part of our salaried compensation package? Did we sign up to test ourselves physically and emotionally, all for the greater good of society? Did we volunteer to put our community's expectations ahead of our own and those of our families? By signing our employment contract, did we agree to forego praise and recognition? Are acts of bravery, heroism, and courage truly just part of the job?

It is basic human nature to want to be recognized, commended, or congratulated for having done a job well. Everyone appreciates praise, a pat on the back. Everyone craves positive reinforcement, whether we outwardly acknowledge it or not.

While my experiences have resulted in some public accolades, police everywhere are doing remarkable things on a daily basis. Those things are mostly not recognized or applauded, and sometimes they are not even noticed. But police deal with the absolute worst kinds of human behaviour and witness horrific things. As a result, we often suffer personally too, either psychologically or physically, or both. Those are the realities. So as a society, we must do better to recognize extraordinary contributions in *every* realm. Furthermore, we must do better to ensure that gestures of appreciation are timely so that their meaningfulness is not lost.

Understanding "Heroes"

In the media and in keynote speaking introductions, I have often been given the dubious title of "hero." I have plaques and newspaper articles attesting to this, but it feels extremely awkward and uncomfortable. While it is an honour, it is also humbling and embarrassing, and I feel like a fraudster.

Several years ago, my elementary school–aged niece surprised me by completing a class project on me; it was a Hero Project, and she had chosen me as her hero subject. When she showed it to me, I was so moved I could hardly read her words on the poster board.

So, what exactly is a hero?

Must one possess superpowers, like the cape-sporting heroes in Marvel movies? Is it someone who bravely defends and protects? Is it a superstar famous athlete?

Is a hero someone who simply gets by? Survives? Someone who does so courageously? With humility? While maintaining some semblance of grace and dignity?

Is a hero someone who does something extraordinary? Perseveres through adversity? Accomplishes great things? Must the results be measurable to lend credibility and legitimacy to the heroic feat? Do others have to accept and recognize those accomplishments before the official title of "hero" is bestowed? And can the title result from a single incident, or must it be a long-term culmination of events?

Can a hero only be borne out of exceptional circumstances? Where can I find the continuum of feats or established criteria that define what a hero must do, which accomplishments or characteristics qualify, for which level of heroism?

My belief is that every single one of us has the capacity and the ability to be a hero. I also believe that heroism shines through more brightly in certain circumstances. We have *all* faced adversity, tragedy, challenge, and those situations force us to act … or not. To some, and even to ourselves, the choices we make about how to react can be mundane, and sometimes don't even seem like choices at all. But I believe that the sheer willingness to persevere despite adversity is truly heroic. We all have that choice. We just don't all *make* it.

Part of my leg may be gone, but my spirit is intact. To those who have looked at me incredulously and told me that they know *they* wouldn't have been able to do it, to have carried on, I offer up that life will undoubtedly throw every single one of us massive, game-changing curveballs. But tragedy and true grit can summon up strength you may never have known you had. If you allow it, it can foster incredible wisdom.

My life has gotten bigger and more meaningful, and my perspective has widened to allow for the uncontrollable change and the inevitable growth that has come with *my* life's circumstances. Simply by living, by carrying on, by trying to slowly move, even though it didn't always feel as if that movement was in a forward direction, I have grown tremendously. I have been forced to reinvent myself around circumstances that I certainly never wanted or would wish upon anyone. But I believe now that no amount of planning can prevent change. All I can hope is that I am better equipped to face what life throws at me with some semblance of grace and humility. I hope that what knocks me down will be overcome by my sheer willpower and stubbornness. I hope I can continue to come back from any future setback as a stronger force, a badass even!

That's become my interpretation of heroism.

Part 3 -

New Realities

Being "Disabled"

I like symmetry. If something is placed on one side of my fireplace mantel, I don't feel quite right until there is a matching one on the other side, and those items should be equidistant from the centre point.

As a former figure skater, I like balance. I like balance in my body, and I prefer it in my surroundings.

So, the sudden onset of one-leggedness, my physical asymmetry, my newly unbalanced life, was challenging both physically and psychologically. My body was a metaphor for my life; it now symbolized my constant quest for balance and order, in my body and in my new life.

And not only was I suddenly and permanently physically asymmetrical, I was also permanently "disabled." I now fit the criteria, the definition. I was now a person "having a physical or mental condition that limits movement, senses, or activities."

Wrapping my head around being disabled was, and often still is, a struggle. It is a struggle because I spend a significant amount of time trying to prove my "abled"-ness. Acceptance of this new disabled status initially was, and continues to be now, a slow and gradual evolution, and that evolution is fraught with pushback, emotional turmoil, reluctance. Often, there were tears, and very occasionally now, there still are.

In the early days of being an amputee, I would frequently forget that I was missing a leg. I would groggily get out of bed and go to step out with my right foot, only to find myself flat on the floor, often with a very sore stump because I had landed squarely on it. I didn't, or couldn't, remember I had to take the time to don a prosthetic leg before walking. Or I would take my prosthesis off while relaxing on a couch watching TV and forget to put it on to stand up. I would collapse into a heap on the floor, stunned to find myself there. Surprisingly, years later I still find myself doing these same things—forgetting that my right foot no longer exists. Even after all this time, my brain simply has not fully adjusted.

Even more surprising is that I still forget that it isn't there despite the constant reminders that it *is* in fact gone. Its absence is driven home to me, on some level, many, many times every single day.

I stumble frequently. I trip over my own feet, one with skin, bones, and muscle, and one made of carbon fibre, metal, and rubber.

I have shooting pains in my non-existent leg. Those phantom pains are worse when I'm tired, and they still have the power and intensity to wake me up during the night. They continue to be unpredictable in frequency and severity, and although I have grown accustomed to them, they still hurt like hell. Even recently, I found myself in tears, desperately begging the pharmacist to give me something to put me out of my misery. I was screaming at God to have mercy on me, asking him how, after twenty years, the torture could be so intense. I was bawling, driving very unsafely through the rainy night, screaming at Him at the top of my lungs, to take pity on me, for fuck's sakes! Have mercy.

I have phantom sensations, like I want to air out the toes that no longer are attached to my body. I want to stretch them, get rid of the mysterious and gross feeling of toe jam.

I get blisters, pressure sores, and ingrown hairs on my bony, atrophied stump. They sometimes take weeks to heal, and while they are often very minor, they cause disproportionate degrees of pain and discomfort. That, in turn, can significantly compromise my balance, my walking, my independence.

I must be hyper-aware of my surroundings, my terrain, making subtle adjustments for sand, gravel, rain, and snow. I watch for tile, hardwood, carpet, and transitions between them. I modify the way my whole body moves for inclines and declines and stairs, and I'm careful about how I use escalators. The adjustments are not natural or subconscious, so the constant need for awareness is mentally exhausting.

I must plan for my day and think ahead about what equipment and footwear and clothing I will require. I deal with volume changes (think: bloating or swelling) in my stump as activity levels and food intake (like too much salt) can affect the fit of my socket. Those volume changes result in me having to carry extra prosthetic socks, fillers to be added or removed depending on varying fits throughout my day.

I must have a heavy, metal shoehorn nearby, at my entry doors, at my bedside, in my purse, and in my vehicle.

I tire easily, and it's difficult to hide when I "hit my wall."

Vulnerability is an uncomfortable place for everyone, and as an amputee, intimacy brought about a different level of awkwardness. Sharing scars and dealing with physical differences is challenging and uncomfortable, so having a sense of humour is mandatory!

I must constantly be ready to jump into show-and-tell mode. Children, by nature, are curious and unfiltered so they ask anything! It is easiest to simply address my artificial leg directly. I explain it, show them how it attaches. I must be ready to talk about it whenever my equipment is on display because questions and stares and comments are inevitable. I don't get to pick and choose those occasions and I don't get to only talk when *I* feel like talking; curious children choose those moments for me. I must be understanding, open (and hopefully lighthearted and amusing) while I address their age-specific questions and comfort their sometimes-mortified parents who are trying to apologetically usher them away.

Leg fittings are time-consuming, sometimes painful. There is always new technology, so I try to ensure I research new products in case a development surfaces that may be beneficial. Legs also require maintenance, periodic check-ups, sometimes frequent trips to see my prosthetist. It is like vehicle maintenance; we require regular tune-ups and occasionally need to upgrade!

I must have modifications done to my footwear so that shoes/boots stay on properly, are comfortable and reliable. A shoemaker adds elastic to much of my footwear. Heels and soles are reinforced or resoled; Velcro and straps are installed. Modifications like these are helpful in increasing my trust in my footwear and building my confidence in knowing where my artificial foot is in space. They are also necessary if I want to be able to wear certain types of high heels or quasi-stylish shoes. And due to my age and stability issues, I will be rocking wedge-style shoes forever, regardless of style trends!

Weight gain or loss can be tough to manage, especially depending on the permanence of those physique changes. For me, pregnancy challenges were significant because my very atrophied, bony stump continually grew and swelled, so my socket (the moulded piece fitted to my stump) kept needing replacement. Pregnancy causes balance issues for most able-bodied women, but for me, falling became even more of a concern during those months. I had to be signed off work on medical leave early during both of my pregnancies because simply moving around presented a tripping hazard. My balance issues in turn impacted my ability to exercise the way I wanted to during those pregnancies, and my weight certainly reflected that! In fact, during my first pregnancy, the day the scale hit 220 pounds was the day I stopped weighing myself (and I still didn't deliver my baby for several days after reaching that embarrassing milestone)!

And there are other modifications I have made to make my disabled life more manageable.

I have grab bars installed in my bathrooms, by my tub, by my toilet, and in my shower.

I sometimes still hop on one foot, though rarely now because I don't hop as precisely or with nearly as much agility as I once did.

I balance on one leg in front of my bathroom sink at night and after exercising so I can cleanse Staub in the sink. I am constantly trying new soaps, antibacterial sprays, cleansers. I experiment with making my own concoctions in efforts to reduce bacteria, prevent sores, and preserve the integrity of my skin.

I use crutches daily, to and from the bathroom, or just when I need a break from my prosthesis. I have devised all kinds of techniques, such as carefully leaning the underarm pads up against a wall or the hand grips against a bathroom counter because, should they topple over, retrieving them from the floor requires the complex combination of one-legged balancing and bending.

Occasionally, when I have a sore or am simply struggling, I use a cane for walking short distances. To practise yoga, I bring a cane with a four-pronged base with me to assist in stability and balance poses. I have canes beside my favourite chairs and my bed to help me transition from sit to stand and vice versa. I recently added a lift chair to my family room and an adjustable-base bed frame underneath my mattress. I have learned that resistance to simplifying life (out of pride, denial, or stubbornness) is downright foolish!

I limit my trips up and down the stairs in my home, so I pile items meant to be transported to another floor in the house on the stairs. Items accumulate so I can take an entire armload each time I make the trek to a different level; it is sensible and preserves my energy. I accept that installing an elevator or moving to a home where the master bedroom is on the main floor is likely in my future.

I have a great deal of difficulty walking barefoot because my prosthetic foot is not aligned for that. I am terrible at walking in sand or gravel or snow because I don't have an ankle or toes to adjust to the instability below my feet.

Because bending over is a struggle and hard on my back, I like things at eye level so I can reach them more easily. As a result, my bathroom and kitchen counters are constantly cluttered. While it makes life more convenient, everything is always a disorganized mess.

I wear a rubber vacuum-sealing shower sock so I can stand upright in the shower.

I have a clothes-drying rack in my bathtub and various drying contraptions in my ensuite so that all my prosthetic components, which require time-consuming handwashing, can be rotated through their turns and air dry after use.

Since I have much of my equipment bedside, my bedroom isn't exactly a "show home" master bedroom. I need various storage and shelving units for first aid equipment, prosthetic parts, and tools.

Driving with my prosthetic leg is painful due to the constant asymmetrical rotation of my pelvis (to apply pressure for the gas and brake), and because I must constantly hover my right thigh slightly off the seat. My back hurts because of the rotation and torque necessary for pedal control. When possible, I eagerly accept chauffeur services offered by family or friends. I suspect that hand-control installation may be in my future.

Driving certain kinds of vehicles can be challenging or even impossible. I am used to the feel of my own vehicle and do not easily adapt to other models. Cars don't work for me due to limited space for my leg to move comfortably from gas to brake. I also find them more challenging to get in and out of, but I also find the angle from the seat to the pedals more challenging to manoeuvre. SUVs and vans usually work well, but I simply won't know until I get in and shift my foot back and forth several times, adjust the position of the steering wheel and seat. Rental vehicles are problematic, and more than once I have refused to depart the car rental parkade before exchanging my assigned vehicle for one I knew was safer and more manageable.

When my children were young, playing with them on the floor was difficult because getting up and down is challenging and clumsy. To combat that, I would often play with them on couches or on beds. I was also extra careful about ensuring my stability and my footing when I picked them up out of cribs, car seats, highchairs, or change tables. Naturally, I was worried I would lose my balance. Since I can't kneel due to the sharp edge of my socket, bathing them in the tub while I knelt on the floor beside them was impossible, so I chose to stand and bathe them in an inflatable tub on the kitchen counter.

Due to discomfort, it is often difficult to get the restorative sleep that is so crucial for daily functioning, but also so essential for pain management. I'm restless and wakeful, and constant repositioning makes it challenging for me to get sufficient sleep. I'm a firm believer that sleep is the most critical element for health, so when necessary, I use sleep aids, both prescription and over-the-counter, and make no excuses about relying on them occasionally. I use various combinations of pillows as props, heating bags, ear plugs, pillow mists, air purifiers, diffusers, salt lamps—whatever helps.

I am unable to keep up with housekeeping, lawn/garden care, and other home maintenance issues that arise, because bending, lifting, and operating equipment quickly exhausts me. I am always on the hunt for lighter, more versatile equipment to simplify cleaning chores, and I incur extra expenses because I hire companies to assist with services.

Changing clothes and footwear is tiring, annoying, and awkward. I lose my balance, I am forced to bend in uncomfortable positions, I need a chair. When shopping, I rarely try items on in store, instead preferring to buy them, take them home and try them, sweating profusely, in the comfort of my own home. It is much simpler to keep receipts for everything and return what doesn't work.

The White family comes from a long line of "sweaters," and I am convinced we sweat more than other people. Maybe our internal temperature gauges are faulty? For me, my sweat primarily comes from my head, so when I exercise, my head and face are drenched. But wearing a prosthetic leg has brought about an entirely different feeling of warmth. I overheat quickly, and since becoming an amputee, I sweat even more because my right leg is covered up with fitted, unbreathable equipment. When the weather is hot outside, I dread going out in it because I know that I will instantly be sweating. That internally generated warmth is accelerated by external weather factors, so there is no escape from the heat. Leg sweat that accumulates can only be addressed by removing my equipment and wiping the stump moisture with a towel. If I don't dry my equipment out, my leg sweat causes my prosthetic to feel slippery and insecure, and I can no longer trust it to support me. For those reasons, dealing with a sweaty stump cannot be postponed, so regardless where I am, whether it be a private or public location, I must find a place to sit, remove my prosthetic, and air out my stump and equipment.

I must travel with extra luggage to carry all my equipment. While it is cumbersome to cart along so much equipment, I must be prepared. I call the airline in advance to ensure there won't be any extra fees associated to bringing a "medical" bag (thankfully, there usually aren't). Extra baggage also requires that I stand in line to check bags because I can't self-tag those bags—an agent must do it. Travelling and being out of my element, without things the way I intentionally and conveniently set them up around me at home, can, in and of itself, be exhausting. I would rather spend time dealing with the issues in advance and bring extra supplies in my suit-case because prosthetic emergencies are certainly not easily addressed on the road.

I get groped by airport security personnel because my leg sets off scanner alarms. Those extra screen sessions are not always done discreetly or respectfully, and sometimes they just make other passengers view me as a nuisance, as if I'm intentionally holding them up. I often notice them rolling their eyes, assuming I am ill-prepared for travel, and have over-looked the clearly defined screening guidelines. Staff members some-times seem inconvenienced at the disruption in flow. Fellow passengers appear curious but are simultaneously trying to avert their eyes. While satisfying security protocols, I am sometimes separated from my kids or travel companions as well as my carry-on belongings, all of which cause added anxiety.

I am questioned and stared at regularly, in airports and any time I wear shorts, skirts, or bathing suits. Those stares are apparent to not only myself, but to my children and family and friends when they are in my company.

Because I have difficulty staying in one static position for any length of time (sitting, standing, lying down), it affects various activities like meal preparation, recreational activities, sleeping, etc. It's a catch-22: physically it is best for my pain if I keep moving, but I have energy limitations that prevent me from being as active as I would like.

I am also very fearful of further injury/physical deterioration, so most of my activities are well-planned and relatively risk-free. I have had to give up some things I love because I worry about getting injured and losing my independence. A simple knee twist or ankle sprain, considered an inconve-nience easily managed by most people—and by me earlier in life—would be challenging for me to handle now. Recovery would be slower.

And so, after detailing all of the above, and as per the very definition of being physically "disabled," I am, in fact, "disabled." I try to do regular things while being cautious, aware, and optimistic. I remain physically active in my own (sometimes) modified ways. I try to accept my realities and the fact that, like everyone, my challenges vary from day to day. I acknowledge what I can and cannot do. I have a handicapped parking decal and I use it so my vehicle door opens widely enough for me to get in. I manage my life mostly well, and although I can never truly forget about it, I try not to let my amputated leg define me. I am in no way "less-than" or inferior because I am "disabled." I also don't wish for or warrant pity.

But I do acknowledge that I am disabled.

Handicapped Parking

One day, I pulled into a handicapped parking spot in an angled lot outside of an outdoor mall. While I possess a handicapped decal, I don't drive around with it constantly on display, so I retrieved it from the console and hung it from my rearview mirror, as required. I exited my vehicle and proceeded towards the store directly in front of my parking spot. A man in his mid-fifties was rummaging in his trunk in the parking stall beside mine. I made eye contact with him and smiled, but he didn't acknowledge me, so I carried on and entered the store. Inside, I completed a speedy return transaction and left the store within five minutes.

The man was still standing by his vehicle, this time with his arms crossed, glaring at me. I continued towards the driver's side of my vehicle and noticed a female mall security guard standing on the opposite side of my van. Right away, the man leaned towards me in a menacing, intimidating way and asked aggressively, "Don't you feel guilty parking there and taking a spot from someone who really needs it?" Taken aback, I realized the security guard had been summoned by him; clearly, my parking neighbour was offended and had chosen to "report" me. Bewildered, I pointed to my decal and said, "Uh, I have my sign up." He was not satisfied and began arguing, so I raised the pant leg of my loose workout pants, exposed my prosthetic leg, and simply replied, "Do you know I have one leg?"

Shockingly, instead of sheepishly backing down, he retorted in an adversarial tone, "Well, you look pretty able-bodied to me!" Still surprised, I responded quietly but deliberately, "Not everyone has a disability you can see, and even people who may look able, might not in fact *be* perfectly able." He paused, lost for something to say. Finally, he said reluctantly, but still arrogantly, "Well, many people use those spots, and they don't need them." I said, "I have a valid decal and I don't mind being questioned, but you should learn not to make assumptions." He shrugged his shoulders and conceded, "Maybe ... " Gathering confidence and momentum and finally overcoming my dismay at the whole interaction, I continued, "It's not questioning me that's offensive; it's your disrespectful approach."

He was still muttering angrily as he got into his car and drove away. The security guard had slunk away, likely embarrassed, wanting no part of the whole episode.

I drove away that day shaking my head and wondering how someone could be so insensitive. I truly don't mind being questioned about using the handicapped stalls and when I do use one, I display my valid decal. My prosthetic leg is often very noticeable because of the clothes I wear. Although I am usually quite mobile, I require my vehicle door to open very widely, something that I often cannot accomplish in a regular parking stall. As an amputee, I also have a significant energy deficit. Sometimes I have bad leg days—painful blisters, fitting issues—and it is difficult to walk. I may have an obvious limp, but I may not, depending on the issue. Sometimes the weather is poor, or the parking lot conditions are treacherous, and the possibility of falling becomes more concerning. I have chronic pain issues. So, while these things may not be obvious to others, I am fully within my rights to park in these stalls.

What bothered me the most, however, about the man's behaviour was quite simply his attitude. He was offensive and adversarial, regardless of clearly being in the wrong. He was completely disrespectful, even when his error in judgment was pointed out to him. I was baffled that he could not simply acknowledge he was wrong, show some humility, some embarrassment, perhaps some compassion? Or better yet, why was he unable to simply apologize and drop it?

It's simple: park in handicapped parking stalls only if you or someone else in your vehicle has a decal. Otherwise, don't. If you have no right to park there, just don't. Don't do it just for a minute, simply because you are just running into a store to pick up your coffee. Don't do it because your errand is sure to be quick, and just to prove it and indicate to people that you won't be there long, you leave your engine running. Don't do it because it is raining or snowing, and you don't want to get wet or wreck your hair. Don't do it because you are just waiting to pick someone up. Don't do it and then stare down at your phone hoping to avoid eye contact with a passerby. Those just aren't valid reasons, and they don't make it acceptable.

Furthermore, if you are compelled to confront someone you believe is being unethical about using these spots, go ahead. Just be respectful, not a self-righteous jerk.

Don't jump to conclusions, don't make assumptions, and be mindful that some relevant information and facts may not be obvious.

Duty to Accommodate (DTA)

When I was working ten- to twelve-hour shifts and had no other responsibilities, I was able to direct all my energy towards work. Unfortunately, my days off were almost entirely spent trying to recover. Wearing my uniform, including my issued boots, my Kevlar vest, and my twenty-pound duty belt, was physically demanding, and keeping the pace was becoming too much. I refused to let anyone know how drained I truly was, but I struggled just to bring myself to work. When I dragged myself through full-time hours, I had very little left in my tank for family, health, hobbies, or fitness. My personal life was also suffering.

To make matters worse, in 2002 and 2003, I had faltered a few times at work. I had stumbled in the snow. I physically struggled to investigate a B&E where there was a large, locked security gate. I had tried to drive a Volkswagen Beetle, knowing full well that my prosthetic didn't fit in it, and had caused a minor, but highly embarrassing motor vehicle incident. With each of these situations, I became increasingly concerned that I might be presenting a safety risk to myself. I hated to admit it, but my confidence in my ability to perform general policing duties was eroding. I appreciated that in those instances nothing devastating had taken place. But by late 2003, I had a baby. I knew that when I was scheduled to return to work after maternity leave, I simply couldn't carry on with the same rigorous work schedule I had had prior to my pregnancy.

Although I wrestled with the psychological piece, I had to accept that, for quality of life and health purposes, *something* had to give. That something had to be work.

As a police officer, and simply as a human experiencing loss, it was devastating to accept the impacts of my new, disabled reality.

I began a series of medical appointments, and it was determined that as a result of chronic back pain issues and the other physiological effects of being an amputee, I should be placed on permanent limitations and restrictions for work. Specifically, I was no longer permitted to do operational police work, and I was limited to twenty-four hours per week. Twenty-four hours equalled 40 percent fewer work hours than a standard forty-hour work week, and that number was based on the extra energy demands I faced. Obviously, these were significant changes, and it meant I fell under federal "duty to accommodate" legislation.

As much as I was acutely aware of my physical challenges, and I was tired from trying to hide my struggles from others, I was surprised at how upset I was by these restrictions. I was fully convinced that it was time I accept my reality; however, in my heart I felt as if I was admitting defeat. I felt betrayed by my body and felt I was a failure. Had everything I had worked so hard for disintegrated? Psychologically and emotionally, I was devastated. Who would I be now?

To me, "duty to accommodate" implied a level of negativity. No longer being capable of performing operational duties, I was told it might be difficult to find positions for me. As a result, I was advised that I needed to "sell myself" to the organization.

Sell myself?

I'm not sure what, if anything, else I could have done, in order to *sell* myself back to my own employer. I had proved myself by passing the P.A.R.E. I had proved myself by requalifying with firearms. I had proved myself by redoing police driving. I had proved myself by obtaining clearance from approved medical personnel. I had proved myself by successfully completing scenario-based training. I came back to work with one leg in only ten months. Many times, I had publicly been called a role model. I had received awards. What else could I possibly have to *sell*?

I had transferred to a new detachment, and my recently imposed restrictions and limitations were not exactly welcome news there. As such, I had no position. I was scrambling, trying to figure out where I could go, who could accommodate me, when I learned that some senior managers felt that my reduced work schedule should be reflected in my compensation. Specifically, since my hours were reduced to twenty-four hours per week, versus the standard forty-hour week, their opinion was that I should only be paid for those twenty-four hours. Their expectation was that I would simply have to forego my salary for the remaining sixteen hours each week. That also meant, however, that my pension and benefits would be almost halved, commensurate with the shorter work week. Clearly, the financial sacrifice, both short and long term, would have been tremendous.

I was then told over the phone by one manager, "Laurie, you can't expect this organization to pay you for hours you don't work." That was followed quickly by, "I work sixty plus hours per week. Don't you think I wish some doctor somewhere would write me off so that I could only even work forty?" I was furious, but speechless. I couldn't even articulate my thoughts. The next comment was, "If I were you, I'd sit down with my husband and do some financial planning."

Years later, my heart still pounds when I recall that conversation.

It is a physiological fact that bilateral below-knee amputees expend approximately 35-40 percent more energy doing daily activities than able-bodied people do. How that translates is this: I'm tired.

Fatigue is challenging to manage. And for other amputees missing more joints or limbs than I, that energy expenditure increases even more. What is left of our body must compensate for the functions of the missing parts.

Having to accept my new DTA status, acknowledging my physical limitations were simply too much for general policing duties, and reducing my working hours to permanently part-time … it was all thoroughly disheartening.

I had sacrificed so much. I had been nothing but dedicated, driven, and motivated. *I* knew how hard I had pushed myself and *I* knew how much I continued to sacrifice for my job. Needless to say, it was insulting to consider "selling myself" by crafting a resume and marketing myself.

As devastating and offensive as I found that initial DTA phase in 2004, I recognize that my thinking has evolved, and my perspective has gradually shifted. Maybe out of choice? Maybe out of necessity. Either way, my outlook today is far more comforting than it was back then.

I was seriously injured at work. After that injury, I did my absolute best to be a productive employee, despite my challenges and ongoing deterioration. Frankly, I busted my ass to *earn* my job back. I deserved that job. *My* job. More importantly, I deserved meaningful work. I knew I had to be flexible, but I also expected that, in return, managers must be creative and cooperative. The bottom line was that my situation was manageable, regardless of some initial, perceived complexities.

Foremost, however, became a focus on my commitment to my personal health. Health is something that, in our youth, we tend to take for granted, but as we age, it becomes more of a priority. We must actively *make* it a priority because it is no longer a "given."

Becoming DTA and acknowledging my deficits and limitations forced to me to revisit what I *could* do. I began to learn to shift the negative self-talk, the shame, the guilt. Instead of hiding my challenges and trying desperately to do what everyone else could, new pathways opened. Those pathways were, at times unconventional, but they materialized, nonetheless.

In some ways, I am fortunate that I knew early on that my health had to come first, otherwise I was incapable of being a good, productive employee, or person. Instead of taking for granted what I always had, I was able to give myself permission to really concentrate on my health, both physical and mental. I could own up to my realities because disabilities in the early 2000s, both physical and psychological, were slowly but gradually becoming a more common and accepted part of conversations everywhere.

Sometimes it meant I had to take time off. Sometimes it meant I had to modify my work schedule. Sometimes I was unable to take on certain tasks or projects. Since I was at a desk, I frequently had to move, wandering around so as not to remain in static positions. I had to learn to give myself permission to contribute differently, and while often that felt like somewhat "less," it was necessary.

I learned that quality of life means much, much more than just showing up to work and using up every last ounce of energy for my job. My family deserved a better version of me. And I deserved that too.

Un-mattering

Most members of the RCMP want so desperately to become a Mountie that once we graduate and officially become one, we eagerly take on that identity. We welcome it with open arms. We earn the title, and we quickly adapt to being a Mountie 24/7. We easily and happily shelve other interests and hobbies and delay life decisions (marriages, children, vacations) based on our postings, our responsibilities, and our commitment to the communities we serve. Our job can take over our existence if we're not careful, and though rewarding, it can, and often does, become too all-encompassing.

In my first few years, I felt as if I made a difference. I was doing meaningful things, making connections, even changing a few lives. Once I became DTA, and my hours and duties were limited, work looked different, much different. In fact, in some of my DTA positions, what I did just didn't really *matter*. It wasn't easy to accept; I was desperate to matter, to be a critical part of a team, to contribute. I struggled and I fought to still matter, but I often simply didn't. At times, when I felt as if I didn't matter, I'm sure some people would contradict that perception; they would maintain that I still in fact did. But I *felt* the un-mattering. It was highly unpleasant and most definitely unsettling. I didn't have the same degree of independence; I had less significance, less influence, less freedom, less discretion, less authority, less impact as a sergeant with twenty years' service, than I did as a junior constable on patrol duties in small-town northern British Columbia.

Initially, I fought the feelings of lack of worth; instead, I committed to being creative. I prided myself on my flexibility and my willingness to say "Yes" to any opportunity. I formed my own relationships and networked within the organization. I liaised with partner agencies. I volunteered for committees and did a significant number of public speaking engagements. But on a far too regular basis, I lacked the feelings that come with accomplishment. I longed for that feeling that comes with contribution, with being part of an effective, results-driven team. Those negative feelings were reinforced more and more frequently, and over time, I simply became tired of asking for rewarding tasks or seeking relevant projects and responsibilities. I didn't relish feeling like a charity case, hoping for someone in a supervisory role to "take pity" on me and give me something, *anything* interesting to do. It was a most unenviable position to be in—to constantly feel like I had to prove my worth.

I became tired of trying. Attempting to demonstrate my value from the sidelines was awkward. Maintaining enthusiasm and dedication became exhausting, because no matter how hard I tried, I felt as if I were treading water. Contributions seemed insignificant and feeling vulnerable was uncomfortable. Slowly, once I learned to accept my circumstances, I realized that not having meaningful work, or "un-mattering," was tolerable. Slowly, it became okay.

Occasionally, I still wonder if things had been different, if I hadn't been shot, where my career would be. I admire my friends and co-workers for their excitement about working on interesting files and having intriguing developmental opportunities. I very much envy their continued success, their rank promotions, their organizational status. I feel twinges when they talk about their career paths, their upward mobility, their opportunities. But I'm learning to create a little distance for myself because those things are becoming more and more distant in my rearview mirror. The wistfulness is slowly fading.

I loved the RCMP and what, for many years, it represented to me as a proud member of it. I have met some of the most outstanding men and women through my work; they are devoted colleagues and cherished friends. The RCMP provided me with some unparalleled life experiences, and the sight of a red serge will forever hold special meaning.

But I am oddly grateful now because I think the gradual un-mattering of DTA, the slow acceptance of what was, and what used to be, helped me transition from my dissipating career into retirement. I believe that despite my phases of un-mattering, in my own way, I did leave a legacy, and with that, I'm finding a level of peace that for many years I wasn't sure would have been possible.

What I believe now is that un-mattering in certain areas, whether forced or by choice, opens possibilities for mattering in others.

God and Grudges

As a Catholic, I went to church most Sundays and I sang enthusiastically in the church choir as a child and young teen. I attended Catholic school and, even during my university years, I often attended the campus mass.

However, when I was shot, God and I broke up. I was the one who broke up with him because, frankly, he deserved it.

I had lived my first twenty-eight years doing *mostly* the right things. Granted, when I was an (occasionally) misbehaving teenager testing limits and boundaries, I did find myself in a few situations warranting minor police involvement (my mom would want me to be truthful here). But I was a good, honest, ethical, moral individual, an individual who, I believed, deserved some basic goodness from life in return.

Instead, I lost my leg at the hands of a pedophile. And when my leg vanished, so did many other things:

- I lost the life I had worked hard to establish.
- I lost my self-confidence.
- I lost my self-esteem.
- I lost my femininity.
- I lost my independence.
- I lost my sense of humour.

- I lost my smile.

- I lost my innocence.

- I lost myself.

People have asked me several times, "Laurie, do you forgive the man who shot you?"

That's a very tough, spiritual question, fraught with all kinds of inner turmoil.

People also ask if I turned to God for guidance and support in my darkest times. That, too, is complicated.

The truth is that, despite my Catholic upbringing and all that I learned as an impressionable youngster, I have in fact *not* forgiven. That honesty may make me a fraud of a Catholic, but I don't believe I suffer any *more* today, decades later, for not forgiving that man for the horrible, senseless hurt and suffering he caused.

I have minimal understanding of the deep-seated issues underlying the decisions that man made that permanently impacted my life. I am also no longer consumed with finding answers. There are none. In the hours between when he shot me and when he was found dead, there was no indication that he wanted my forgiveness. In fact, I believe that during those hours, he felt he was justified in his actions. To him, I deserved what I got.

For me, forgiveness must be warranted. I would like to believe that if a person who wrongs me feels remorse and truly desires forgiveness, I will in fact forgive. Since that is not the case in my shooting, I don't forgive. And I most definitely do not forget.

I acknowledge that these admissions are far from virtuous or honourable. After all, we are regularly reminded that forgiveness is for ourselves, for personal growth, and that we will never reach our ideal version of ourselves if we do not selflessly rise above. In this instance, I disagree. I don't carry with me a heavy, unbearable (or even burdensome) load of anger that prevents me from having a fulfilling life. Contrary to what some might say, contrary to what so many motivational quotes preach, and contrary to how many people I know feel about the topic, letting go and forgiving is *not* the only key to authentic happiness. I have let go and I have moved on. I just haven't forgiven, and I don't believe I'm worse off for it.

I have evolved since my initial breakup with God, but my relationship with him still ebbs and flows. For years after my trauma, I was like a hateful ex. I was pissed. I wanted no part of God or religion, so we didn't "talk." I gave him the silent treatment because having faith had clearly done me no good. It was just easier to cut him out of my life.

I dreaded when people assumed it was my strong Catholic faith that had carried me through the darkness, and when confronted about it, I would have to confess the truth. They were so wrong, and they were/are always surprised that in such a time of strife, I chose to run away from the church and my spirituality, as opposed to running towards it. But I felt abandoned by God. I struggled with my faith, my beliefs, and all the things I had been taught as a child.

However, when I got married in 2002, I did feel the need, the obligation, and the desire to get married in a Catholic church. I was compelled to do the pre-marriage course with my non-Catholic husband-to-be. Despite my emotional distance from the church at that time, I still felt a sense of familiarity in the church and going anywhere else would have felt ... wrong. I knew then that I was evolving because even my fractured relationship with God couldn't deter me from making that decision. To me, it was a peace offering of sorts. It was me opening my mind and stating to God, to myself, that I was cautiously optimistic about possibly, maybe, at some point in the future, finding a place of peace, of acceptance, and resuming my Catholic ways. It symbolized hope.

In the following few years, both of my children were baptized Catholic for the same reason ... just in case.

Today, my children know little about the Catholic religion, and it occasionally embarrasses me that they come from such a different place than I. I struggle to do justice in explaining Christmas and Easter to them because they don't have Catholic school and church reinforcement. For example, at Christmas when my son was very young, he thought that the nativity scene and its characters on display in my parents' home was a great setting for his superheroes to wage battle. Spiderman and Ironman would protect Baby Jesus while various underwear-clad WWE wrestlers were the bad guys trying to blow up the manger. The three kings went to war trying to save the farm animals, and it was all-out chaos. I loved seeing my son's imagination at work and I was greatly amused, as were my fellow Catholic family members. I was also overcome with guilt, guilt that he would never have the understanding that was ingrained in me as a child.

My simplistic rationale was that I felt that bad things should generally happen to bad people. I felt that in my law enforcement world, where I saw people breaking the law and choosing to do awful things to others, the crappy life stuff should be doled out in *their* direction. I had a highly naïve "reap what you sow" attitude. I mean, shouldn't bad things happen to bad people, and good things happen to good people?

Admittedly, those are questions I still contemplate from time to time. I would like to say I am now so much more mature, and wise, and don't still feel somewhat … *shafted*. But I can't. Don't get me wrong, I have many wonderful things in my life, and I'm well aware my circumstances could be *far*, far worse. I *know* I have so much for which to be grateful in my life.

What it boils down to is that I held a grudge. For a long time. Call it juvenile or petty, but I prefer to call my honesty self-actualized, evolved. Either way, my relationship with God continues to slowly change. Maybe we will arrive at a place of understanding, peace, and mutual respect for each other's position. For now, I take comfort in the gradual rekindling of a relationship that for my first almost twenty-nine years was a foregone conclusion, as well as a powerful guiding force and a compass. I continue to talk to him and pray in my own unconventional way, and for now, it works for us. We are hashing out our differences and redefining our relationship. We are moving past the deep-seated grudge I held against him for so long. We are even slowly reconciling.

Survivor's Guilt

Survivor's guilt is defined as guilt one feels because of having made it through traumatic circumstances when others did not; it is a concept that in 1998 instantly became highly relatable. I felt it constantly in the early days and, more frequently than I wish, I still do. I believe it's why I cry when I watch the news or hear stories of tragedy. It's why I dab at my eyes when I read about other people's heartache and grief. It's why I get choked up when I see people struggling. It's why I feel compelled to help when I can, to fight for justice in small ways. I take on other people's challenges in a more profound way than I ever did before I was shot.

Survivor's guilt is also why I'm overcome with emotion when I walk by a large poster display in my rehab facility; the pictures and the story chronicle my return-to-work journey.

In the early days of rehab at G. F. Strong, I wanted to see women pictured in framed photos around Ricky's office. The only ones on the stark walls in the basement office were of young adult male amputees climbing mountains and skiing down beautifully groomed runs. There were Paralympic athletes and gorgeous models missing limbs. There were beautiful people doing extraordinary things—or simply looking at me while just being beautiful.

But where were the photos of people not really being ... exceptional? Where were the photos of people to whom I could relate? People that were more ... average? More ... normal? People who weren't setting out to conquer impressive feats of athleticism? Feats that I hadn't even been interested in tackling as a two-legged, able-bodied person? Where were the people who would never walk a runway or grace the pages of a sports or fashion magazine? Where were the people who simply wanted their old lives back? Where were the people who wanted their ordinary, maybe even mundane lives back, those same lives they had often complained about but were quite comfortable with? Where were the responsible adults who simply went to their jobs every day, who worked out at the gym to stay fit, and occasionally rollerbladed around town for fun? Where were the recreational golfers who liked to take a power cart once in a while so their cocktails wouldn't spill? Where were the people who longed to lace up their skates and breathe in the familiar and comforting smells of the ice arena where they skated with their adult synchronized skating team? Where were the people who happily played beer league softball in the summer and curled recreationally in the winter? Where were the people who were happy to go to a pub with colleagues after work and have a Bacardi white rum and Diet Coke? Where were *those* ordinary people? Where was *I*? People like me weren't on those walls.

So, I complained about that injustice from the first time I went into the prosthetics clinic. I would sit there trapped on the treatment room bed, legless for long periods of time, staring at those posters, while I awaited prosthetic leg adjustments taking place in an adjoining room. I would look from Staub to those walls and question my future independence, something I had always taken for granted, and I would resent those smiling faces. How dare they conquer such lofty goals?

Ironically, however, not that many months later, I became that ordinary, normal, unexceptional person, the one whose smiling face, for a time, grinned down from the wall at RCMP "E" Division Headquarters in Vancouver. I am the one whose face still graces a prominent wall in the hallway at G. F. Strong, a hallway that countless patients and family members and staff members pass by daily. I became that subject, the person on display. I became a *relatable* success story because my goals were not to climb mountains or compete for gold on an international sporting stage. I was there motivating other patients, inspiring them to overcome adversity, to face *their* challenges, to take back a tiny morsel of their power. But that photo display, as proud as I was, and still am, of it, at times in those early days felt hypocritical; hypocritical because it was and is difficult to look at those pictures and know that when some of them were taken, I didn't truly believe in myself. I know that, in spite of the looks on my face in many of those photos, inwardly I was still hoping to crawl away and quietly disappear from the world.

To this day, I stop in my tracks when I'm visiting G. F. Strong because that poster, that photo series, represents a highly tumultuous personal journey. Even though I am often still recognized more than twenty years later, I prefer to silently, and inconspicuously, watch current patients and visitors stop in front of my poster. I watch them read the words and study the photos of my rehab and back-to-work process. They appear impressed, fascinated, and inspired, and I am proud, yet conflicted. I'm conflicted because I don't want some of those people in the unfortunate states in which some of them have found themselves to feel bitter or resentful. I don't want them to focus, like I once did, on impossibilities, things that could never be. I don't want them to feel my accomplishments are impossible for them in the same way that I perceived the beautiful athletes and models that used to almost mock me from the same walls.

I am proud of the hard work, the determination, and the perseverance that have brought me to where I am today. But I admit that I also feel guilt—guilt that I lived, that I made it out of the hospital, out of rehab, back to my job, back to many parts of my life. I am so fortunate that I was able to move forward and realize some incredible milestones that for a long time seemed out of reach. Yes, I made it out, while some others, well, they just don't. Or they do but they are forever changed irreparably—physically, mentally, or both.

I have no idea why I was one of the lucky ones.

I didn't know it in 1999, but I do know now that because I was given another chance, because I survived, and because I was given a chance to thrive, I owe it to myself and to everyone else who loves me to create the best life possible—the very best life possible *for me*, in spite of my circumstances.

To those athletes and models who once gracefully decorated the walls of that building, know that although I never aspired to do what you did, I was ultimately inspired by you to do what was right *for me*; it doesn't include red carpets, gold medals, heli-skiing, or rappelling a rock face, but I thank you nonetheless!

To those patients at G. F. Strong who have passed by my poster, I hope that you too can accomplish whatever is achievable for you. Be ordinary or be extraordinary.

Just find peace by doing and being what is right for you.

Chronic Pain

When I began physiotherapy in January 1999, I hurt. Staub hurt, and the nasty, long wound I had from groin to knee on my left leg was very painful. My body had been so weakened that everything was a struggle. My upper body muscles were fatigued from the crutches. My armpits were raw and chafed. My hands blistered, then calloused, from the rubber grips. My back was achy from the asymmetry in my newly disabled body. My sound leg (my left side) was becoming increasingly strong because it was now my singular source of support. Understandably with two legs, body weight is typically shared approximately 50/50 between your right and left side. However, with only one full leg and foot, that sound leg was slowly but constantly learning to overcompensate for the non-existence of the other. My quad and calf and hamstring were working constant overtime.

As time wore on, pain changed. The pain in my stump slowly and steadily decreased. As I gradually learned to walk on a prosthetic leg, my dependency on crutches became non-existent (save for night-time bathroom trips or sore leg days). The strain on my left leg lessened gradually as I learned to bear weight on my right leg. Regardless, my right leg muscles, which had until recently been so strong and defined and capable, shrank in front of my eyes. But while the atrophy occurred at an alarming rate, I was slowly learning to trust my right side again. I adjusted to a new level of normal, and over the course of several months, most of the major leg-related pain gradually reduced to a more manageable level.

Back pain, however, is constant. I sought chiropractic assistance in the early days, and my physiotherapist often worked on my back. However, the pain that began in those first few weeks in late 1998 has never, ever gone away. In fact, over time it has become more and more pronounced. I have had several diagnoses over the years, and nothing appears to be serious enough or worthy of surgery or major intervention. Sacroiliitis, degenerative disc disease, disc bulges, arthritic change, inflamed facet joints, etc. The details of the issues and the specific diagnoses are virtually irrelevant and frustratingly minor in justifying the total impact they have on my body. My pelvis is always slightly rotated and torqued. My shoulders compensate for the discrepancies, and my lower spine appears to be compressed, slightly twisted to the right and upwards. My core is rigid and unable to relax. My neck is constantly stiff. Driving exacerbates the pain issues because I drive with my prosthetic leg. In order to brake or accelerate, I manipulate the prosthetic foot by shifting my pelvis and hip, thereby creating stress on the lower back. When I ascend or descend stairs, my propulsion is not equal on both sides because I do not have an ankle to flex and a calf muscle to contract. There are many daily activities that cannot be modified to ease the discomfort, and despite being an accomplished amputee "walker," many subtle imbalances simply cannot be fixed. Mechanical issues are unavoidable; it is as frustratingly simple as that.

What is more significant, however, is the considerable impact that chronic pain has on quality of life. Living with chronic pain is *exhausting*. The level of pain fluctuates but it is *always* there. It is there every moment, every day, year after year. Moreover, as the time wears on, I reach new plateaus of "normal." Periodically, I am forced to accept that the level of pain I am in is now never going to be reduced, regardless of what measures I take. Pain is simply a constant state that periodically worsens. I cannot remember what it is like to not hurt.

Living with chronic pain naturally impacts personal relationships, and it certainly negatively impacts intimacy. It compromises my moods, causes physical fatigue, and can most certainly be a root cause of depression. It is exasperating for those who love you; they want desperately to help allevi-ate the pain, or even just to minimize it, but they are mostly helpless.

I have many pain management strategies and am always searching for new options, but mostly what is most effective is to try to "ignore" the pain. While I would *never* suggest that pain management is a simple mind-control issue, I do find that distraction techniques are beneficial for me. Staying busy and keeping occupied, physically and/or mentally, help me the most. If I can stay occupied as much as possible, it *somewhat* diverts my attention and helps keep the gnawing, unrelenting pain issues at bay ... sort of. I can't eliminate them, but earlier in my day, I am better equipped to prevent them from completely overtaking my existence. However, in spite of my best distraction techniques, pain regularly and far too frequently launches itself into the forefront and often, depending on factors like mood and fatigue and intensity, simply cannot be ignored, and no amount of distraction helps at all. I believe that accepting the fact that I'm in pain and acknowledging its existence doesn't mean I have given up, succumbed, and allowed it to take over and "win." It doesn't mean I'm being negative or pessimistic or a complainer. It just means that it is my reality, and it needs to be addressed. That means finding coping skills is critical.

Chronic pain is not easily explained. It seems nebulous, mysterious, unbelievable, even fictitious, because in some cases it is hard to pinpoint specific causes. People can be judgmental and expect that I should simply "get on with it." "Seeming well" backfires, yet admitting I'm in pain can make me feel like a failure for apparently not having the internal fortitude or the basic will to overcome it. Some people don't believe that pain is actually real. They believe it's psychological, or an attention-seeking technique, or that the person is simply choosing to be a victim. People in pain are sometimes not believed if they "look well." (I don't believe that physical appearance should be a factor, but studies have shown that it can be.)

Chronic pain is a gradual loss, and as I age, new challenges surface. It forces me to constantly adjust to, and accept, new and unwelcome states of normal. It requires constant adaptations, adaptations I absolutely do not want to make but must. If I opt to pretend my issues don't exist, I feel that I'm being misleading and untruthful. If I accept and acknowledge those issues, I feel as if I'm being selfish and narcissistic.

I acknowledge and accept my physical limitations; however, I'm not at an inordinately increased risk of injury. By no means am I looking for sympathy. I just must face the fact that pain accompanies everything I do, whether moving or still, and I hope that others won't judge me based on an issue to which they may not be able to relate. I don't necessarily expect others to understand my situation. I just hope that they refrain from making assumptions about my capabilities or lack thereof.

A couple of years ago, some girlfriends participated in a muddy obstacle course race, and I absolutely ached to join them for the camaraderie of a girls' weekend away. I wanted to enjoy the social interaction, and as a former athlete, and someone who enjoys competition, I really wanted to do the course. But I knew right from the initial wine-induced conversation that I was out, unable to participate. I didn't want to miss the fun, the adrenaline, the laughter, the female bonding, but I had to remind myself of the realities of such an adventure. For one, I hate to be dirty, so that helped me reconcile the decision not to go—although that has absolutely nothing to do with chronic pain! I just don't like dirt and I especially don't like dirt on me. I knew that my prosthetic leg would get dirt in it and would likely need some maintenance. I also hate running just for the sake of running. But I love sports and games and belonging, and I could not bear to simply attend the girls' weekend and just spectate. Passively. I miss being truly active and I love challenging myself physically, so it's just not in me to watch such an event from the sidelines. I'm too competitive, too social. I knew I would be sad, enviously watching, and wishing things were different. I knew I was not capable of hiding my feelings well and I knew I wouldn't truly be a part of the total experience. So, I bailed. Wisely, I recognized that knowing myself, and accepting my limitations, demonstrates compassion for myself. It is sometimes unpleasant and sometimes means missing out on fun, but it's necessary for taking the best possible care of myself.

It's difficult to accept that maybe, just maybe, pushing through pain is not always possible. I have stayed up many nights crying, wondering how I could be so tough in some circumstances, yet unable to recover from the chronic pain. I mean, hell, I took a bullet! I remained conscious for four hours afterwards, bleeding extensively, experiencing excruciating pain, wondering if I were about to die. I endured relentless, unbearable phantom limb pain for months. I laboured for several agonizing hours before my first child was born via emergency C-section. I would suggest that my threshold for pain tolerance is high; therefore, shouldn't I be strong enough to make a solid mental decision that I can handle pain? Can I not simply *will* the pain away? Could I go so far as to persuade myself that it is simply a figment of my imagination? Maybe I can convince myself chronic pain is not even a real concept! Because the slightest acknowledgement of its existence seems like failure, a moral weakness, a massive character flaw, a conscious choice to give up and let the suffering beat me—in essence, accepting that I am a helpless victim and have given myself permission to continue to wallow in that defeated state.

I feel defensive and occasionally don't feel like I'm taken seriously, so it makes me reluctant to talk about it with certain people. I get tired of talking about it, and I am definitely tired of thinking about it. But the pain is there. All the time. It never goes away. *Never.*

Post-traumatic Stress

In 2003, I became pregnant for the first time and began to grow at quite an alarming rate. I was stumbling more and more frequently due to the added balance challenges of my quickly expanding body. I was eating soda crackers while horizontal in bed in feeble attempts at fending off the "morning" sickness that plagued me all day and night. Despite those unfamiliar experiences, I was absolutely thrilled at the fact that I was going to be a mom!

I was caught up in my new nesting activities, painstakingly choosing bedding and furniture and car seats and swings. I was trying to envision my new life and anticipate my needs as a disabled new mom. I spent hours wondering how my life would soon look, what equipment and modifications I would require to simplify my life and my yet-to-be-established routines.

Since I had been taken off work early in my pregnancy due to problematic balance and overwhelming fatigue, I had even more time to become caught up in the what-ifs about my future. The problem was, I soon realized, that I had extreme difficulty envisioning a future. I couldn't pinpoint the reason, but I could not plan like I once could. I couldn't see past the immediate future, and I had no ability to look long-term. "Oh well," I reassured myself, "It must just be part of being pregnant."

During that time, I had a home visit from a Veterans Affairs Canada (VAC) case manager, because RCMP officers injured on the job qualify for benefits under a Veterans Affairs program. I had been receiving benefits for a couple of years, but I had never had a home visit, so when the case manager called to schedule the meeting, I was reluctant to agree. I wasn't quite sure of his role, and I had become very private and protective of my personal space, so I was uneasy about having a stranger in my home. I was newly married and newly pregnant and was spending a lot of time alone. I wanted to focus on all the good that I had in my life, and I knew that any VAC conversation would revolve around my disabilities. I didn't want to feel bogged down by the past and have to talk about *those* issues. I didn't want to revisit my shooting, my traumatic story. I wanted desperately to move on and be present for this new, joyful chapter of my life. However, naively I thought that if I did not agree to this meeting as requested, I might inadvertently sabotage my eligibility to continue receiving those VAC program benefits. Since I relied heavily on them, I felt I must be fully cooperative. I agreed to the visit.

When the VAC representative arrived, he toured around my home, and we discussed my ongoing medical issues and needs. I knew he wasn't an occupational therapist, and I knew he wasn't assessing my home for possible modifications or recommending more suitable daily living aids; I was pretty up-to-date on both of those topics. We had a lengthy dialogue about my history, my day-to-day activities and routines, and I dutifully answered every question. Finally, the case manager looked at me squarely in my eyes and said, "Have you ever been assessed for post-traumatic stress disorder?"

I looked at him blankly. I knew nothing about PTSD. Zero. I told him, no, I hadn't been assessed. He nodded knowingly, then gently, but strongly, suggested I look into it. He departed and left me there wondering what I had said or what he had seen, either in me or in my home, that had led him to that conclusion.

I was confused but my interest was piqued, and I immediately went to my computer to Google PTSD. The first thing I found was a short quiz to assist in PTSD self-diagnosis. Although I recognize that Google searches surrounding medical issues can cause fatalistic thinking and inaccurate diagnoses, I knew I needed to proceed.

Quiz questions revolved around such things as:

- Are you jumpy? Irritable? Easily startled?

- Do you have sleep issues?

- Do you have difficulty concentrating?
- Do you withdraw from social events? Do you avoid certain experiences?
- Do you experience flashbacks?
- Do you have distressing memories?
- Do you relive your trauma? Do you have nightmares?
- Do you have unexplained anxiety? Sweating? Hypervigilance? Muscle tension?
- Do you feel inexplicably sad? Detached?
- Do you depend on alcohol or drugs for pain relief?
- Do you have difficulty visualizing the future?

To some extent, my answer in every single case was … YES.

I sat there in disbelief. Then I became emotional as reality began to set in, because making those acknowledgements was painful and I didn't want to admit any of it.

But YES.

I went back over the quiz several times trying to convince myself that I had to be wrong. There was some sort of mistake. Yes, I had been injured on the job. Yes, the injury had been traumatic, and the fallout was very serious, but I was better now. Wasn't I? In fact, I was as "better" as I would ever be, and I was no longer "injured."

But unfortunately, the more often I read the questions, and the more I studied the possible answers, the more I could not deny my reality. I became more and more acutely aware that everything I had been experiencing since November 1998 might finally make some sense.

It slowly became clear—the depressive tendencies; the fitful sleeps, often involving horrible nightmares; the baseless rituals I simply *had* to engage in several times a day; my jumpiness; my interest in being alone; my preoccupation with safety; my inability to look to the future; and more. It all began to sink in. It was starting to make sense.

Tears were streaming down my face. I was trembling, overcome with fear and anxiety about what it all meant. But at the same time, I felt somewhat relieved to know that there may in fact be a name for all the things I was finally admitting to myself that I was experiencing.

Maybe, just maybe, if there was a name, along with an actual diagnosis, based on sound medical reasoning, facts, and science, I could start handling my issues more effectively?

I immediately made an appointment with a psychologist to discuss my revelation, but prior to that first appointment, I was conflicted for days. It was an internal tug-of-war. I was hesitant to confront my issues and pursue this diagnosis. Did I really need to obtain official confirmation that I, in fact, was a true sufferer? What good would dwelling on the past do? Isn't that what counselling would be about? After all, I was a newlywed and expecting my first child. Wasn't I supposed to be happy, blissfully content? Shouldn't I be focused on the good in my life and the impending birth of our child? Shouldn't I be overcome with excitement, happiness, joy?

But I also knew I needed answers and more effective coping strategies, and I knew I couldn't manage my issues alone. I had been struggling, and was still suffering, for five years since the shooting. Now that I felt I had identified the root cause of my issues, I knew I would be doing myself and my husband and our soon-to-be new baby a disservice if I didn't try to fix some of my problems.

So, obligingly and full of dread, I drove to the periodic counselling appointments and painfully relived my experiences and my struggles, session after session. Each time I left feeling exhausted and weepy, wondering what I was doing going down this path, why I was looking backwards. I felt worse, and frankly, the process was pure torture. I felt weak and unable to manage my life. I felt trivialized when the therapist recounted a story about how he himself had felt when he'd been bitten by a dog while delivering newspapers as a twelve-year-old. He hadn't been injured but tried to draw parallels between that experience and my shooting. The process left me frightened and vulnerable. I felt physically ill, often nauseous. In fact, I felt many things, and none of them were positive.

After each appointment, I would strategize about how I could comfortably cease going, how I could cancel my next session and escape the process. But deep down, despite all the negativity, I felt like I owed it to myself and my family, so I persisted, appointment after painful appointment.

Together, the therapist and I analyzed my physical and psychological behaviours, my responses, my reactions, my coping strategies. And one day, unsurprisingly soon, my initial suspicion and subsequent conclusion were confirmed by a health care professional. I received the official diagnosis.

I had PTSD.

Post-traumatic stress disorder is a mental illness. By definition, PTSD is a psychological response to experiencing trauma involving death or the threat of death, serious injury, or sexual violence. It causes intense fear, helplessness, horror. It can affect anyone, regardless of age, culture, or gender. It can vary in intensity and can surface months or even years after the trauma. It can also last *forever*.

I felt oddly validated when I initially received that diagnosis; it had a real title, one based on extensive research. But I was terrified. What did it actually mean for my life? Where was I to go from here? Could I be cured? Fixed? How would I manage? How would I be perceived now that I officially had a *psychological disorder*? Now that I had a *mental illness*?

Early in my career, before my own tragedy, I recall attending my first fatal pedestrian motor vehicle accident. I remember the dark night a few weeks before Christmas. I remember seeing the victim's shoes, empty in the roadway. I remember being momentarily confused as to where the body belonging to those shoes could be. I then remember seeing the victim's lifeless body, many, many feet away from his shoes. I remember my naïve curiosity at how the incident had happened, how it had resulted in such devastation and chaos. I recall the utter disbelief I had that the impact between vehicle and human had caused the victim to be launched so far away while his shoes remained virtually in their tracks. I will never be able to unsee those empty shoes. I will never forget the sights and smells of the autopsy that followed.

Before my own traumatic hospital experience, I remember what it was like to accompany vulnerable sex assault victims for rape kit exams at the hospital. I remember those victims sharing the trauma they had been through. I remember their pleading eyes looking at me, hoping I could spare them from more pain, more humiliation. Their eyes begged me to spare the loss of their last shred of dignity by having to expose themselves and their private parts to strangers. I remember feeling helpless that I couldn't prevent them from feeling more violated by subjecting them to this investigational necessity.

Before my shooting, I recall the first time I had to notify next-of-kin of the death of a loved one. I recall the face of the woman and her child as I explained to them that her husband, her child's father, was dead. I remember mentally rehearsing, trying to find the right words, knowing that there were none. I remember the pit in my stomach when I had to share that not only was her husband dead but that he had committed suicide. I remember her scream. I remember her collapse in the entryway. I will never be able to unhear that shrill voice.

Those moments, though handled professionally at the time, impacted me deeply. They were emotional experiences at the time, yet when I think of them now, as a person with PTSD, I feel an even more heightened level of sensitivity. It's as if there are pre- and post-shooting versions of events; facts remain the same, but the attached emotions are more profound. I wonder if I handled the "people" side of those situations well. I wonder if I showed enough compassion and empathy. I wonder if, had I had the life experiences then that I've had now, I would have done anything differently. I truly hope that I did everything I could do and did it to the best of my youthful twenty-something abilities in those unforgettable moments. I hope that in those life-changing, devastating situations, I was sympathetic, compassionate, and caring and … humane. I hope those things because I now know that moments like those can be indelible, carved in our brains forever.

It is impossible to be a police officer, to carry out our duties and remain detached. Most police officers choose this profession because we are community-oriented and want to help. We want the world to be a better, safer place. Yet we are human beings, and it is human nature to feel emotion, to feel compassion, to feel empathy. We can't do this job and simply choose *not* to feel while we are on duty. While that would be a most beneficial adaptation skill and useful while at work, it is impossible and unfair for anyone to expect that from us. We can't simply turn our humanity on and off as required, contrary to what many members of the general public expect.

PTSD affects every single area of my life. As a person who has PTSD, I am hyper-vigilant and anxious. I check my surroundings constantly and any sense of retraumatization, revictimization, instantly sends me back to the intense physiological state I experienced when I heard that "POP." My body's reaction is to go into fight or flight mode. Adrenaline is released. My ears still ring. My heart still pounds so quickly and loudly I can hardly breathe. I can't think straight or distinguish between imagination and reality. My senses become keener, and my awareness of my surroundings is heightened. Muscles tense up. I shake. I still feel panic.

I am always aware of my environment and the possible inherent risks. If there are no apparent or obvious risks, I simply resort to creating my own! I am excessively concerned about safety, and unfortunately for my children, my concern, which prior to their arrival used to be only for me, has now spread to them.

My PTSD triggers can be anything that brings back memories of my trauma or an association to another upsetting occurrence that took place at some time since then. These triggers and their effects may sneak up quietly and gradually, or they may come in and slam me like a wrecking ball. They can be subtle and sometimes not even recognized as such in the moment. It sometimes takes hindsight to comprehend that my reactions in a past moment were even in fact PTSD-related. But these triggers can also be paralyzing, suddenly freezing me into an almost immovable state. They can make me catch my breath, stop in my tracks. They can wake me from sleep. Whatever intensity, they can come spontaneously, at any time, with no notice or identifiable, justifiable reason.

PTSD involves a pure, physical reaction, along with a psychological reaction. It extends far beyond reason or rationale; no amount of sheer willpower or determination can stop these reactions from ever starting in the first place. No amount of mental resolve or discipline or fortitude can ensure that the debilitating, frightening effects of trauma will never, ever resurface. The effects cannot be wished away. They can be unpredictable and irrational and uncontrollable. And they can be very, very unfair.

Months after I was shot, I received a package in the mail while I was living in my condo in Vancouver. It was uplifting to think that there would be some gifts, some encouraging cards, or some bits of much-needed motivation inside the parcel. Those parcels still arrived in the mail intermittently, and I appreciated them immensely because they boosted my spirits after gruelling days of rehab.

This day was no different; the parcel's return address was that of the Kitimat RCMP Detachment, and after an exhausting day at physio, I sat down to enjoy opening it. As I tore back the wrapping, I saw a clear, plastic bag bearing the familiar marks of a police exhibit bag. In horror, I realized that the hiking shoes I had been wearing when I got shot were sealed inside that exhibit bag. Worse, because the bag was still sealed from the evidence locker, the shoes were still covered in my blood. I panicked, heart racing. "What could I do?" I couldn't just throw them in the dumpster! They were bloody, and the exhibit bag had the police file number and the caption **"White – Attempt Murder Of"** in bold black letters. I burst into tears, hastily threw the sneakers into the washing machine, and cut up the bag into a million pieces.

Those shoes were a trigger, a huge, highly upsetting one. To this day, that brand of shoe reminds me of that terrible experience, that moment at which my life instantly divided into two parts: the part before I was shot and the part after I was shot.

Anniversary dates can be challenging; inevitable associations are drawn to the meaningfulness of them. Some years I hate November 27. Some years I'm able to celebrate it by making a conscious decision to look at my life through a positive lens and actually succeed in doing so. Other years, even if I am in a good place personally and make an intentional, conscious decision to be positive, I end up wanting to skip the day entirely and advance the calendar page. Sometimes, despite the passage of time, the date can be borderline unbearable. Some years are tougher than others, but there is no formula or stage of life that helps predict which years will be worse. In recent years, I have chosen to use that anniversary date to decorate for Christmas, to make a concerted decision to focus on being grateful for another year, another birthday (which comes three days after my shooting date). Some years I choose to do positive things—I donate blood, I donate money to a special cause, I do something to pamper myself. Each year brings its own challenges or peace; I just don't know which it will be until the day arrives.

Sometimes, out of nowhere, I begin to shake for no reason, and my fine motor skills seem to disappear. I can't write. I drop wine glasses. I can't put on mascara. It feels as if I'm right back in that vulnerable moment, reliving the actual physical shock and the trauma. I hear the noises, the words that were spoken. I can't identify a trigger.

Occasionally, I see a vehicle that resembles the one that was beside me under the carport when I was shot. Sometimes I see a stranger with similar features to the man who shot me—a similar physique or similar hair. Sometimes I'm jolted by someone's eyes resembling his; I knew his beady, hate-filled eyes because they had stared at me in July 1996 when I had arrested him for impaired driving. They were also the same eyes that bore into me while he resisted that arrest, while he fought with me and my partner. They were the same eyes that glared at me for hours afterwards while he refused to provide a breath sample. They were the same eyes of the venomous man who, in his final hours, felt compelled to pen a letter addressed to *Cunt*stable White. To me.

Sometimes out of nowhere I smell an odour that brings me back to the gunpowder, the smoke, the burning flesh, or the antiseptic smells of the hospital rooms that followed. I work hard to silence the pervasive negative thoughts that creep in.

I make lists and calendar reminders even for simple things. I make them because I like being able to cross something off, even one or two minor or trivial things, to make me feel as if I've accomplished something. Anything quantifiable. As a person with PTSD, acting on a simple reminder to make a phone call and talk to another human or remember to pick up chicken from the grocery store can be a monumental feat some days.

On other days, maybe as a distraction tactic, I become almost manic and unstoppable, ticking off many things, no matter how insignificant, in short order. During those phases, I don't sit still. I can't.

Sometimes I feel compelled to avoid relaxation simply out of fear of having that downtime. I know from experience that unwinding can backfire. It may not bring peace; it may simply offer up an opportunity to relive painful reminders and visit dark places.

Some nights I hardly sleep, and I rarely feel rested. I am a light sleeper and am always awake before my children quietly wander towards my room on the carpeted floor and reach my wide-open door.

Very occasionally, I am irrationally afraid of the dark. Bedroom doors need to be open. House doors need to be locked, and the house alarm needs to be set. Nightlights are mandatory. When I'm outside at night, my head swivels like an owl's as I shoulder-check and constantly survey my surroundings. I regularly mentally rehearse what-if scenarios and self-defence tactics.

Sometimes I procrastinate falling asleep because I refuse to close my eyes. Closing my eyes can feel like punishment, because I'm left alone with my thoughts, my fears, my imagination. I wonder if the man who shot me planned it for a long time. I picture what he was doing before he pulled the trigger, what his true intentions were. I have flashbacks. I relive what happened, sometimes with different outcomes, some better, some worse. I wake up feeling physically spent, but I welcome the dawn and the start of a new day, despite the exhaustion.

With PTSD, being awake can be stressful, but falling asleep can mean nightmares. I wake up panicked and sweating and flailing, sometimes trying to fight off a bad guy. My bed will be soaked, and I am an emotional wreck. In those moments, I have difficulty distinguishing between reality and what I have just vividly witnessed or participated in during my nightmare. I dream that someone is chasing me, trying to kill me, get revenge, trying to "finish the job," so to speak.

My sleep issues can certainly wreak havoc in relationships. It isn't easy to explain to someone else why I'm not sleeping restfully, why I forego personal privacy to have to have the bedroom door open, why I feel I have to be prepared for fight-or-flight at all times. Sleeping in other environments like hotels or friends' homes creates a whole host of distressing new worries—unfamiliar darkened areas and strange noises.

Sometimes I feel an overwhelming sense of loss. I have deep sadness, and some days, for no obvious reason, I am tearful, caught up in grief.

I have difficulty concentrating and I try to laugh off my distractions, my frequent changes of subjects, my random, discombobulated trains of thought. I sometimes feel the need to address them, acknowledge them, to normalize them as part of my … lovable quirkiness! On my computer or phone, at any given time, I have several screens open simultaneously because I cannot focus on any one task for long periods of time. It's a visual representation of my brain!

It takes me age to read novels—sad for a formerly voracious reader. I often read the same page over and over before I digest what's on it. Before 1998, I could sit down and devour a book in a matter of days, even hours, but sadly, I am not sure I have even read a book, in its entirety, since then. I simply no longer possess the concentration skills required.

I worry incessantly and have a heightened sensitivity to other people's trauma when I hear about it or see it on the news. I feel grief and sadness and loss in a different way than I did before experiencing my own trauma. I feel empathy and an odd sense of camaraderie even when I don't personally know the victim. I subconsciously draw parallels between their situations and my own, even if I can't relate to specifics of their story. Details don't matter because I feel their grief and their pain. I relate to the sheer victimization. I then take it a step further. If I hear of a fire, I become focused on potential fire hazards and safety precautions I must take in my own surroundings. If I hear of a boating incident, suddenly water sports seem to be hazardous, irresponsible activities. If I read about sex crimes or domestic violence, I'm suddenly pre-occupied with how I can better protect myself and my children. Any stories of accidents, grief, or loss stir up these heightened sensitivities. I try to ignore them or, at best, keep them at bay, because I know full well that they are disproportionate, irrational, and not applicable to my life. But they are powerful and flare up suddenly and at unpredictable times.

When my children were younger, I had to face spontaneous and innocent questions from them. I had to be truthful and tell them that I lost my leg because I was shot, yet I wanted to ensure that they felt safe, that their mommy was fine. Unfortunately, offering this reassurance can feel hypocritical; after all, I was shot, and being shot kind of shatters the whole "this world is a safe place" thing. We want desperately to protect our children, to keep them from harm, to fix any and all problems they encounter. It's natural, and after all, isn't it my job, as their parent, to equip them with tools to go forth into this world with confidence, with reason, with awareness, with optimism? And feel … safe? Yet I know for a fact that the world is *not* always a safe place. There *are* inescapable dangers. But I have to ensure that *my* fears are not imposed on my children, and that they don't develop irrational anxiety that prevents them from venturing out, participating in life, and creating their own experiences. It's hard to actively disallow my realities, my personal experiences from negatively impacting their ever-changing and developing perspectives.

Having children exacerbated many of my PTSD symptoms because my own issues were suddenly transferred onto them. My circle of people to worry about expanded and, by extension, lent a little more credibility to my anxiety.

I have routines and rituals that I must exhaust before I feel comfortable. I must be confident that the garage door is shut, doors are locked, curling irons are off (even if I didn't use them), water faucets are off, stove is off. I will check any, or all, of these things several times before each and every departure, several times per day. While backing out of the driveway, my children will watch our garage door and chirp out, "It's closed!" Frequently, I depart our home, confirm the garage door is closed, drive up the street and out of our neighbourhood, then turn around and return to reconfirm the garage door is in fact down. I have even called on neighbours to enter my home after I have left to be sure that certain appliances and faucets are off. I need my mind to be put at ease, and no strategy I develop can effectively silence the irrational worry that I *may* have overlooked one of these matters. I have tried taking pictures of the closed garage door and the unplugged curling iron, and I have tried doing pre-departure tasks in a systematic order, but none of those brings enough peace of mind.

I am a stock-piler. I buy multiples of everything—toilet paper, deodorant, dish soap etc. It took me a long time to figure out why I did this, and when it finally became clear, it was very unsettling. People who suffer from PTSD feel an impending sense of doom, and for me, because I had come so close to dying, I had taken that fear and begun subconsciously preparing for when I was no longer here ... for when I was dead! To me, for example, that meant when my children needed diapers, and I got "low" (to me) on supplies, I had an overwhelmingly irrational sense of anxiety. Therefore, replenishing that supply of diapers immediately became of paramount importance.

I hate being in confined spaces like drive-thru car washes. In public places, I try to sit facing other people so I can keep an eye on what's happening. I always have a planned escape route. I loathe crowds and *despise* people infringing upon my personal space. Large concerts or festivals can be unbearable. I panic if I feel I'm trapped. I loathe highway tunnels; as I approach them, my chest tightens, and my breathing becomes shallow. I have to sing out loud or phone someone to talk to me, to distract me, whenever I go through one.

Sometimes, for no logical reason, I am overcome with the irrational feeling that everyone and everything is an enemy, a bad guy. I have to engage in calming self-talk and actively tell myself to take deliberate breaths to cope with these odd situations. I know it isn't reality, but it feels as if my body temperature is rising and there's an instant reverberating noise in my ears. It's as if the world is closing in and I am overcome with a sudden, strange, overwhelming impulse to get away. The problem is that I'm not certain who or what I'm trying to avoid. I just know I'm desperate to escape from everyone.

COVID-19 has added another layer of anxiety to my worries about safety; before I was wary of human enemies, but COVID-19 has made me wary of other, more invisible dangers.

I cannot watch TV shows or movies with any kind of violence or drama, or with too much tragedy. When the tension builds and someone is inevitably going to get shot or stabbed—the type of music preceding those moments is a dead giveaway—I know a terrible, graphic scene is imminent and I panic to shut the TV off or change the channel, plugging my ears while averting my eyes.

I used to be extremely social; turning down an offer to do anything with other people was rare. I am no longer that person. I certainly can be social and extroverted, but my PTSD makes me long for alone time. Unfortunately, it makes me isolate myself too much because I feel pressure to be "on" when I am socializing. I want to be charming and light-hearted and engaging, but sometimes it's easier to choose to just withdraw. I go into avoidance mode, avoiding friends and colleagues and small talk as much as possible. This isolation has caused problems for me in my significant post-shooting relationships; my desire to be alone can easily be misconstrued as disinterest.

Because of the unpredictable nature of such PTSD triggers, I make many changes to avoid situations that may exacerbate symptoms, and I try to plan as best as I can, for those situations I cannot avoid. I am better equipped to recognize triggers and the impacts PTSD have on me. It's a relief that I'm considerably better at coping now.

I admit that when I began therapy, I believed that someday I would be "fixed." I viewed PTSD as an injury, one that over time, and with proper care, would heal. But long ago I arrived at the conclusion that I don't think I will ever be "fixed"; there is no such thing for me. I've grown and flourished in many ways, but PTSD is simply part of me, part of my personality. Managing it, and its effects, will be a lifelong challenge.

I am proud of myself for having had the courage to speak publicly about PTSD, to state what I know many other people are afraid to state. I did it, and continue to do it, so that I can show understanding and compassion for an issue that is shrouded by shame, guilt, fear, and pain. I want to continue being a student, an active participant in dealing with my own stressors. I want that because in dealing with my stressors head on, I can welcome growth, improved resilience, adaptability, fulfillment. I want to help reduce stigma. I want to be vulnerable so I can help promote aware-ness, to remind people they are not alone in their struggles.

Depression

I have battled depression a few times in my life, even before I was shot. In fact, the first time was just months after I graduated with my master's degree at twenty-three years old, living back at home with my parents. Juggling four jobs kept me extremely busy, but unbeknownst to me, my mental health was gradually deteriorating. Being unable to line up a job in my field, combined with the student debt I had incurred, made me feel like a failure. That was extremely difficult to accept, given that I felt I had done everything "right."

Months went by and my life didn't look at all the way I'd anticipated. I was slowly but surely becoming a shadow of my former self. I became extremely thin because I was on the go, and food had begun to make me feel nauseous. If I ate, I often vomited. I knew it wasn't intentional, and I knew I didn't have an eating disorder. In fact, it was highly inconvenient, so it just became easier to not bother eating in the first place. Frankly, it didn't matter because I wasn't hungry anyway. I cried regularly, more and more frequently and unpredictably, often in the car in between jobs. Finally, one day, my mother came home to find me lying in a heap on my bed. I was sobbing uncontrollably, and it was the only time someone else had witnessed the depth of my despair. I was embarrassed to be outed by her, but I was also beyond caring. At my mom's insistence, I sought help from a close family friend who also happened to be a well-respected psy-chiatrist. Fortunately, over time, with medication and counselling, I was able to regain some perspective and become healthy again.

I detail that pre-shooting depression experience because that time in my life changed me profoundly. It showed me how quickly and drastically I could spiral downwards, how depression had stealthily crept up on me. I hadn't been able to recognize the gradual changes as they were occurring. I couldn't see the impact those changes were having on me, my behaviours, my personality, my life. I didn't see them while they were happening, only the results … well after the fact.

As I look back now, I am grateful for what that experience ultimately taught me about myself. It taught me how to familiarize myself with my own personal signs and symptoms of unwellness. As a result, I'm now much more aware of subtle negative changes within myself. It also made me aware that at certain times, problems are simply not managed well alone. Help is available and, at times, necessary. I was fortunate that my mom found me crying that day, and now I have developed enough self-awareness to recognize those low times myself. I know that when I do have those phases, I have developed resilience to handle them better, and courage to get help. That initial experience helped de-stigmatize the idea of asking for psychological assistance. That experience also happened so early in my life that it, along with increasing societal awareness, has made it easier and easier for me to reach out when I need to, to feel confident in knowing that I *can* get through those dark times.

I don't feel ashamed to admit that I continue to see a psychiatrist. In fact, I feel quite comfortable admitting that I continue to seek professional help navigating the physical, emotional, and psychological challenges that life continues to hand me. I feel that seeking medical advice for any condition, physical or emotional, constitutes excellent self-care. My psychiatrist's expertise is specialized, unique, and effective. He helps me cope with historical events, my Operational Stress Injury, as well as evolving daily pressures. The support I receive from him is different from that offered by my many close family members, friends, and other support systems.

I am also not ashamed to admit I have relied on medication at various times in my life for periods of depression. I don't know if that first experience in my early twenties made me more susceptible to experiencing depression later, after I was shot. What I do know now is whatever strategies I've used seem to be working for me; I haven't required medication for depression in many years.

What I also know now is that sadness is *not* the same as depression; there is a significant difference between the two. I know the difference between my own sadness and depression and PTSD reactions, and knowing those differences continues to be tremendously helpful in coping with day-to-day pressures and stressors.

Part 4 –

Relationship Matters

No Regrets

I have always been an analyzer, a what-iffer, a strategic planner, and naturally, those habits lead to long sessions of second-guessing decisions I made in the past. We all wonder about possibilities had we taken different paths.

Dr. Passey, my experienced and oh-so-knowledgeable psychiatrist, regularly reminds me that there is no such thing as regret; as he says, no reasonable person makes a consciously poor decision. Therefore, every decision I make is based on the information I have at the time I make the decision. I weigh my information, I analyze, I brood and lie awake at night stewing. When I finally make that decision, I am confident I make it carefully and with the best of intentions.

So why then, do I allow new information and new experiences, along with time and distance, to convolute my thinking? It's unfair to view my previous decisions through new lenses, with a current and much different perspective. I ruminate, I resort to catastrophic thinking, wishing I had done things differently because surely, had I done *that*, the results would have been much different, and *much* better.

The problem is that I cannot judge what I have done in the past. If I knew then what I know now, yes, I may have done things differently. However, I didn't have the luxury of having those experiences and information *at that time*. I did the best I could. I remind myself that I am a reasonable person. This is just one of the ways counselling has shifted my thought patterns.

I am learning to be fair to myself, to quit beating myself up with woulda, coulda, shoulda. I am learning to stop the judgments and allowing myself to be at peace with my decisions, whether the outcome was ideal, or what I envisioned, or not.

"Regret" is slowly being erased from my vocabulary.

Happiness and Goalposts

When I was in the throes of new parenthood, and my marriage was beginning to crumble, I had an unpleasant conversation with someone I considered a friend. During that conversation, she said, "Laurie, from the outside looking in, don't you think everyone thinks you have it all?"

That comment was ironic in many ways, laughable in others. And it enlightened me.

I had worked hard to regain my life post-shooting, to establish a new normal. My desires involved a picture-perfect, double-income family and a beautiful home, complete with an actual white picket fence. From the outside, and in theory, I should have had it all. And yet I didn't.

I have realized that I often set unrealistic goals for myself. I, like many others, gradually convince myself that if I obtain a certain position at work, if I am in a relationship with a certain kind of person, if I own a certain object or product, if my children are successful at a certain activity and performing well academically, I will finally have "arrived." I believed that attaining those things, achieving those goals, should equal happiness. It is all just a matter of getting "there."

I no longer view things in the same flawed way.

I know now that my wishes, hopes, desires, and dreams frequently and rapidly change. I set my sights on things and people, and when I am close to "acquiring" said things and people, I shift my sights onto other things and take little pride or comfort or joy in achieving my goals. I subconsciously move the goalposts, so success becomes less meaningful, less appreciated.

I have also realized that once I reach my goal, I feel I *should* be happy. I think that since I "got" it, whatever the "it" is, life should now be perfect. When it isn't, I used to become deflated. I would be frustrated because despite having what I thought I wanted so desperately, I was sometimes still unhappy.

Contrary to what I was once told by someone important in my life, I *don't* think the grass is always greener somewhere else. I just think that, for me, when I am approaching *my* "finish line," I have already accepted that what-ever it is I'm after is already mine. When it becomes within reach, it no longer represents the priority or the lofty goal it once was.

More importantly, I have realized that "there" is not a tangible end state. Happiness isn't about simply achieving status or wealth or material things. Regardless of how we are perceived by others on the outside looking in, goals are only measurable by our own personal yardsticks.

Homes with white picket fences are not trophies; they certainly don't symbolize having it all. I now know better than to judge those superficial things. I also no longer want to put things off until I get "there" because what once was "there" is actually my *here*.

"Fuck Bad Word"

In 2006, when my son was one and my daughter was three, we relocated from a city I adored to a much larger one four hours away. We left a home and neighbourhood I loved, and friends I cherished. To make matters worse, I was just coming off maternity leave, and my employer was in no rush to assign me a new position. All the uncertainty exacerbated an already highly stressful situation. The move had come about on short notice, and since my marriage was already on shaky ground, I felt very much alone. The relocation transfer occurred due to a promotional opportunity for my husband, and since we had a young family, I hoped that perseverance would see us through. I wanted desperately to believe that once the dust settled, we would come out the other side of the upheaval and change in a stronger, more unified place. An engagement, a new house, a wedding, an almost instant pregnancy, an infant, another new house, then another infant, all in the matter of a few years, had presented many welcome and joyful distractions. Those distractions, however, both highlighted and dis-guised our relationship flaws. Some of them were magnified, while others seemed to periodically disappear.

A mere six months after moving to our new home, in a new city with no friends or extended family, my husband and I split up. In my heart I knew it was the only way forward, but that didn't make the reality of it any less terrifying or devastating. It was utterly overwhelming and very, very sad. I was filled with grief, but oddly, I also felt liberated in a way that was uncomfortable to admit. My "million-dollar family" had disintegrated, and I no longer had to live in a difficult situation, but I felt shame that I felt a certain relief.

Unsurprisingly, the unravelling of my marriage left me in a very undesirable predicament, and I found myself in a lonely, shared parenting arrangement. That arrangement meant that I was forced to spend half of my nights alone while my beloved kids were spending time with their father. I desperately wanted my children in *my* home, with *me*, *every* night; after all, I had entered parenthood expecting it to be a full-time commitment. But now, with two parents at two different homes, that full-time parenting schedule was no longer an option.

My husband and I drew up a separation agreement ourselves, divided our assets, carefully negotiated our individual time with our children, and slowly began establishing our new routines. I had the kids beginning on Wednesday. I would keep them through Saturday one week, Sunday the following. When my children were on their dad's watch, I would work most of my hours, and occupy myself with errands and chores. Mostly I was marking time until I could excitedly collect them on Wednesday and fall happily back into full-time momming. As each weekend drew closer, I would begin to dread the upcoming drop-off at their dad's. While their dad is a devoted father, I loathed giving my children over to him every few days; I wanted so badly to keep them to myself. Practicality would set in each week though, and I would make the twenty-minute drive to his house and agreeably trade them. I had no choice but to set aside my selfishness and operate in their best interests. Children are not possessions, and their needs come first, *not* mine. Their needs include their dad.

During the days when my children were with their dad, I was left with a significant amount of alone time. That time largely revolved around guilt. I truly hadn't known that the act of becoming a parent would make me question every single thing I did or didn't do. I had no idea of the degree of guilt I could carry, and that guilt was exacerbated on kid-free days. Most parents fret about safety, nutrition, health, grades, activities, and sleep. I certainly did all those things too, but would take it a step further by pondering such things as:

Should I have stuck out my marriage to avoid this cyclical pain?

Was that "F-bomb" I dropped going to be repeated by one of my children at school?

Why didn't I *fight* for more time with my children?

Are my kids being damaged by this parenting schedule?

Am I doing everything in my power to minimize the disruption of the back-and-forth trips they make between their dad's house and mine?

Are other people judging them for coming from a "broken home"? Does having divorced parents automatically make my children less whole? Is my marital status somehow considered a risk for them to be chosen by others to be a friend? Those eyerolls and whispers by other adults, are they insinuations or affirmations that we are all somewhat "less"?

Is my commitment to parenting, and ultimately to my children, somehow minimized simply because I share them with the one other person who loves them like me?

Am I doing them a developmental disservice to discourage/disallow sleepovers at friends' houses? (Side note: Am I the only parent who loathes sleepovers?)

Am I smothering them, hogging their time while they are home with me, hoping for fewer scheduling commitments on "my watch" because I miss them so much when they're gone? Is it wrong that I don't want to share them more than I already must?

Should I be increasing their responsibilities around the house? Am I coddling them and letting them "off the hook" because I prefer to do fun things when they are home with me instead of making them do chores?

How do I balance important life lessons with fun and quality family bonding time? How does that balance occur when my time with them is limited because I share them with their dad?

The questions continue even now. Some of my concerns are admittedly common, probably universal. Others, not so much. As my kids age, some questions change. Others don't. The worry, the anxiety, the guilt, and concerns about their overall well-being, however, remain.

As a parent, I have come to realize that I feel my children's pain far more deeply than I ever would have imagined pre-parenthood. When they are rejected, *I* am rejected, and I draw parallels to my own life experiences. When they face a particularly difficult social situation, I vividly recall the emotions I felt when I was called "the new little fat kid" in Grade 2. When they don't have sporting success, I recall the embarrassment and disappointment I felt when I failed my skating tests or was cut from teams. When they weren't invited to a birthday party I felt those familiar feelings of isolation, of being left out of social gatherings.

In those early single parenting years, I was often looking for signs, for reinforcement that I was doing ok, that I was, in fact, operating as a reasonable, moderately successful mom.

One day, thanks to my son, I received such a sign. I strapped my children into their approved car seats, and we headed down the street in our van. Now, I'm a rules-y mom. If there are rules, standards, they *must* be followed. I like order, I am pre-occupied with safety, and I like consistency. Although my strict adherence to rules, self-imposed or externally determined, has been the source of much ridicule within my family, it is the way I feel I function best.

My three-year-old son looked out the window and saw a child on a skateboard. His eyes instantly widened. This skateboard-riding child did *not* have his helmet on! My son, dumbfounded at such an obvious oversight, stated in disbelief and disgust, "*So* not safe, Mom, *so* not safe!"

I nodded emphatically in agreement, proud of his observation. Amused, I said, "You're right, Brett. *So* not safe."

We proceeded on our way, and I looked in my rearview mirror at him to see a thoughtful look on his face. He then said, "Stupid bad word, Mom."

It dawned on me where this was going. My son was reminding me of the rules his three-year-old mind knew. At daycare, he was not allowed to use the word "stupid." Brett wanted to demonstrate to me that he was learning his rules.

1. Wear a helmet.

2. Don't say "stupid."

I replied approvingly, "You're right, Brett. Stupid is a bad word."

Proudly, I continued driving. Brett was "getting it." Although that positive parenting reinforcement I longed for was coming in unpredictable ways, I could take *some* credit in these successes, couldn't I?

Ten seconds later, my son, looked out the van window and said triumphantly, "Fuck bad word too!"

I was speechless. That was his third rule.

3. Fuck bad word.

Whether he heard that word from my mouth or from his dad's (likely both!), I will take those three lessons as wins!

Like many single parents, I face challenges.

I have no backup. I have no family locally. If I'm stuck or inconvenienced because of leg issues, I am unable to drive any of us anywhere.

Thankfully, I rarely become sick, but when I did and the kids were small, I didn't get to lie around and feel sorry for myself. I had to get kids to school or activities. If I was having a bad leg day, I didn't get to take a day off. When they were younger and one of them was sick, both had to come to the pharmacy, doctor, grocery store, ER. That made *all* of us grumpy, but I couldn't show *my* grumpiness. I was expected to be positive and upbeat, and have coins for the candy and water machines, along with activities in my purse to occupy them.

I'm Santa Claus. I pretend to go to sleep when the kids go to sleep, but instead I lie there praying I will stay awake long enough to perform my duties, my alarm set for 1 a.m. as insurance. I wait, not so patiently, to ensure they are sound asleep, so I don't get busted making forty trips up and down the stairs. I carefully place gifts under the tree, all the while with a heightened sense of hearing. I don't want to get caught or be the one to ruin the magic.

I'm the Easter Bunny and I'm responsible for the Easter treasure hunt tradition. Rhyming couplets must increase in difficulty to align with the kids' improving reading and comprehension skills. Since the objective is to make them run from floor to floor, from room to room, up and down stairs, as much as possible, I go through the hunt myself, methodically and quietly placing the clues in order. Any mistakes mess up the entire hunt, so it is critical for me to do the hunt myself the night before Easter to avoid any potential morning confusion.

I'm the Tooth Fairy, albeit sometimes not a very good one. When my daughter was once at her father's house, she lost one of her first few teeth. Upon her return to my house, she announced that she had gotten $30 for it—$30! I questioned her extensively about it and couldn't believe how high her dad had set the bar for tooth fairy payments. Geez, with two children and many future lost teeth between them, it was going to be a costly process! I then decided to give her my wallet and ask her to show me how the Tooth Fairy's payment had been made. Without hesitation she chose a toonie and a loonie. Three dollars, not thirty—whew!

A few times, the Tooth Fairy was unaware of tooth loss. A few times it was just an oversight and the kids forgot to remind me. A few other times, the kids intentionally didn't tell me they lost a tooth because they were suspicious about Tooth Fairy operations and legitimacy. They schemed together, to see if the Tooth Fairy would, in fact, do her job. On those mornings, when no money materialized because the Tooth Fairy was not aware any money was owed, I became creative. I consoled them by blaming their excessive night-time kicking and flailing. I quickly found a toonie and assisted in the all-out search for the coin that *must* have been lost in the sheets or fallen under the bed. I strategically hid the coin in my hand

and carefully placed the "lost" coin within the bed sheets or in and around the bed. And so, the magic continued. For a time, the kids believed that if they left their tooth in a cup of water beside their bed, the colour of the water they found the next morning would indicate the dress colour of the fairy that had made her night-time appearance. I bought food colouring and would stir the water to ensure a lovely fairy-ish colour. And, to up the intrigue even more, I sprinkled glittery makeup on the water's surface. Oh, the joy on their faces when they discussed what the fairy must have been wearing to leave such a beautiful display!

In years when the kids are not with me on a holiday or a special occasion, we simply celebrate on a different date. If the kids are not with me at Christmas or Easter, I resort to trickery. I set up the gifts as if the Easter Bunny and Santa Claus showed up, and I send pictures of their haul awaiting them at home. One year we were visiting my family out of province at Christmas. It made no sense to transport Santa gifts in our luggage, so I arranged for a friend to set up the gifts under the tree and send photos. That way, the kids could be excited about their return home, and there was no way to suspect I had played any part in the Christmas Eve activities.

Since there is no other adult around, when it was my birthday, or Mother's Day, I would buy a cake for myself on behalf of my then-too-young children.

I also swore that just because I was a single parent with a prosthetic leg, I would never be the pajama-wearing school-dropoff mom. But morning chaos was unavoidable, and I *was* her … often!

When there is shared parenting, involving considerable driving and shared responsibilities, there are trade-off challenges.

Did we remember all their sports equipment? Their homework? Backpacks? Are their favourite items in there? iPads? Books? Clothes?

Who is completing the notice for the field trip? Has the money been submitted? What about hot lunch? Oh, and the activities, sports, and lessons—did we register by the deadline? It's never-ending.

Forgotten items increase our guilt, and that guilt equals extra drive time, but their dad and I don't even consider the inconvenience because we recognized years ago that it isn't easy for them to go back and forth between our homes. We always go out of our way to ensure the kids have everything they need. We will make the trek to the other house to retrieve a longed-for forgotten skirt or preferred pair of shoes. We will backtrack to retrieve a forgotten device. And because of the back-and-forth nature of their existence, items such as school backpacks, musical instruments, sports equipment, and favourite clothing are never unpacked. They are constantly in-transit and never actually find a permanent storage place in our home.

Having two households also inevitably leads to curiosity about how things are at my house versus how they are at their dad's. What's different? What's the same? What's good at each place? Where could we improve? In the very early stages, it was tough to refrain from trying to "one-up." I quickly (and thankfully) realized that while it's natural to want my kids to be happy in my home, focusing on having "more" things or "better" experiences is unhealthy. We *want* them to be happy at both places.

I feel fortunate that my divorce was amicable. My ex-husband and I recognized that, while we couldn't remain married, we could make shared parenting work. A few mutual friends chose "sides", which was an unfortunate reality for everyone, because choosing sides is often unnecessary. Sometimes people assume that they will be put in an awkward position and pre-empt what they perceive to be inevitable conflict by addressing it prematurely. When we originally split, a couple consisting of friends of both of us, told me in no uncertain terms, that they would not pick sides. However, their actions in the following few months made it apparent that they in fact were choosing a side. And it wasn't mine. It stung, but it was reality.

Despite my willingness to dissolve my marriage, and despite knowing fully well that doing so would unquestionably alter my day-to-day circumstances, I will never be able to fully describe the pain of watching my family—my ex-husband and two precious, tiny children—walk away from me in a parking lot at a football field. It was symbolic of so much—like when I was shot, I felt as though I had been kicked out of my life.

I will never be able to articulate the depth of the sadness I felt the first time our children drove away with their dad, their stepmother, and half-brother, leaving me to face the emptiness of a too-large home.

Each time the kids left, I struggled to tidy the toys, the strewn-about clothes: they were mildly comforting reassurances of the kids' *never*-quick-enough return to *our* home.

However, despite the challenges of sharing parenting, their father and I are both role models in our own rights. Our kids are loved unconditionally, and we each put our children first. We are flexible with scheduling and the kids are always welcome at both homes. Our kids know they do not have to choose one over the other, and while they miss the parent they are not with, they don't have to feel guilty for enjoying their time with the other parent. We offer our children different environments and a variety of experiences. We are all simply doing our best.

So, despite coming from what some would call a "broken home," both of our children are loving, caring, bright, and compassionate human beings. Our circumstances have taught us all many, many lessons.

With my two favourite people!

And "fuck" is still a bad word.

Protesting Tutus

When my daughter was three, she wanted to wear a tutu every day. Every. Day. At first I tried to discourage her. It wasn't logical. It wasn't weather-appropriate. She would have to wear tights with her tutu. It wasn't practical. But she would stubbornly protest. Every. Day. I felt she was being defiant and silly, but finally, instead of resisting her and stifling her individuality and her fashion choices, I allowed it. Initially, I still felt annoyed, and I would sigh and shake my head when she walked down the stairs wearing yet another skirt. Then one morning I realized that while I had a certain expectation in my own head, the truth was, I didn't actually mind what she wore. This was *my* silly issue, not hers. So, I helped her with her tights. I sent trackpants with her in her daycare backpack so she could put them on to play outside. And guess what? She was excited. Mornings went more smoothly. And I was happy. She was expressing herself, wearing exactly what she wanted.

I realized that allowing my daughter to be free to make her own choices was not only good for her, but it was also great for me. She was establishing herself, identifying what she wanted, and there was no solid reason for me to oppose. Not allowing this issue to define how we started our day was a huge step in learning that I am not always right, my position on things doesn't always make sense, and that others have choices as well—even three-year-olds.

To take that a step further now, many years later, I miss the tutu, princess-y girly-ness. In hindsight, seeing my daughter revel in who she was, establishing her independence and taking pride in her careful clothing selections, was powerful to witness. I want to be like she was (and still is). I want to own my choices, make decisions that make me happy in the moment, that show off my individuality.

I am going to do more of what makes me happy, because my overall health, both physical and psychological, is *my* responsibility.

And while I have no business wearing tutus, I want to present myself to my world the way my tutu-sporting three-year-old did—confident and owning it!

Cultivating Confidence

When my son was three, we were in a busy grocery store lineup when he decided to make a sudden announcement. He looked at me and announced loudly, "I have big penis!"

Some moms would be embarrassed; I am not one of those moms. I burst into laughter, as did several (but not all) of the people around me.

I look back on that moment and wonder about the two ways I could have handled that awkward experience. I could have been embarrassed, humiliated, and chastised my son for being inappropriate. I would then be expected to apologize to those who heard him boast about the size of his … "package."

I, however, chose to laugh and to praise him. Although I was surprised at his sudden statement, I decided my best bet was to encourage him and build his confidence by saying, "Yes son, you sure do!"

I viewed that situation as an amusing but great confidence builder for him, and we laugh about it to this day.

While my tendency is to be self-deprecating and minimize compliments, I am slowly learning to give myself permission to accept them with a simple "Thanks." While I have no desire to make boastful announcements in public places, I need to continue developing my own confidence so I can be proud of myself, my gifts and my attributes, in ways my three-year-old son showed me!

The Toll It Takes

Not long after becoming a single parent, I faced having four circulation procedures. With increasing frequency, post-amputation, I would experience a strange and very sudden pain in my stump. It usually happened within an hour or two of waking up and getting upright, but curiously it didn't happen every single day. It was occasional at first, but over the years it increased to four to six mornings each week. The more often it occurred, the more I was filled with dread at the very thought of it happening. I would become very anxious and wonder if I would experience the pain, or be lucky and have a day off.

The pain was excruciating, as if someone were torturing me by tying a tourniquet around my knee and shutting off my circulation. My stump would become red, then purple and very hot. My face would be pale, and my heart would pound. The only answer was to take my leg off and simply wait it out, not a convenient solution when driving or walking into daycare or work in my dress clothes. So many times I would have to pull off to the side of the road in a panic to take my prosthetic leg off! I would stop my van, jump out, and pull my pants down or skirt up, not giving a damn who saw, because the desperation for relief was overwhelming. It was inexplicable, but I knew that if the pain hadn't happened by 11 a.m., I was fortunate to be escaping it entirely for that day.

The phenomenon was difficult to explain to my doctors. After all, the inconsistency was confusing. Was it a leg-fitting issue? Was it a result of pressure? Why couldn't I reproduce the sensation? Why did it only occur in the mornings? Why did it only happen on some days and not every day? What I did know was that it was unbearable, and the panic it induced was complicating the situation even further.

Over the course of a few years, my vascular surgeon tried a few techniques in attempts to address the issue. Those procedures varied in how much recovery time they required, but all were very challenging, since I was unable to wear my prosthetic leg afterwards. I felt so defeated facing periods of compromised independence.

After one such surgery, I was trying to corral my children upstairs for bedtime. I was in terrible pain and couldn't have been more eager to take my leg off and lie down. After I'd made the painstaking trek slowly up the stairs on my crutches, my two-year-old son decided he did not want to go to bed. He tore off down the stairs and looked up at me defiantly, flat out refusing to come back up. No amount of pleading would make him change his mind, and I was on the verge of a meltdown. Tearful and flustered, emotional and angry, I looked at him through my blurry eyes and begged him one last time to *please* come up, trying my damnedest to negotiate with him through my woeful, please-take-pity-on-me eye contact.

He refused.

My four-year-old daughter, who had witnessed the whole episode, recognized the pain and the physical struggle I faced. She looked at me distressed, and said sadly, with a heartfelt attempt at a reassuring grin, "If I was bigger, I would go down and pick him up and carry him up here for you."

Tears that had been somewhat controlled until that point began to flow freely. And moments later, thankfully, my son gave in and miraculously came upstairs of his own free will.

What I realized that evening was that I hadn't been giving my young children enough credit. They had shown me that they were far more perceptive than I expected. Even though children are, by nature, very self-absorbed, they are more in tune with our feelings than we think. At a young age, they are able to process some of the challenges we face and the toll those challenges take on us.

Best Available

When searching for concert seating, I am all for scouting out the "best available" seats, and when shopping, naturally you will choose the best of what is out there. Relationships, I have learned, however, are a much different story.

In some instances, recognizing that we are "settling" can be difficult. When there are few options in dates, or friends, we find ourselves settling for people who don't necessarily meet our standards. We allow ourselves to dismiss the absence of certain characteristics or behaviours, simply because we desperately want someone compatible. Mandatory qualities we would have previously looked for in new partners or friends can fade in importance. When we're lonely, dealbreakers are ignored or minimized because our loneliness status gives us permission to assign them a lesser degree of importance.

Many years after my divorce, and more than five years into a different relationship, the combination of a series of medical and work matters, along with an unexpected and devastating break-up, launched me into very unfamiliar territory. I ended up off work, reeling from the stress. I lost about thirty pounds, trembled constantly, found myself drinking a lot and barely eating.

I was so sad. I was excruciatingly lonely. I was also lost, because it had taken me more than five years to finally believe that the relationship I was in was right for me. In those five years, we had weathered finalizing our respective divorces, his cancer, an unexpected marriage proposal (I was caught off guard, wasn't ready, and said no), and countless other issues. Through it all, our pre-existing friendship, established many years before our romantic relationship, had prevailed. I had learned to trust and had given myself permission to move forward, maybe even plan a future.

It was a big step since PTSD makes imagining the future difficult, but I'd finally arrived at a place where I could begin to see possibilities. Then I was handed a devastating setback, by way of an unexpected break-up.

Over time I realized that, when it came to that relationship, I was happy … enough. But there were also reasons I had been unable to move forward, faster. I believe now that I was opting for the best of what was available. We loved each other, we were compatible and enjoyed each other's company, but there was something missing. Work stressors, medical issues, struggles with self-worth, lingering feelings of shame over my marriage/single parent status—all those things made me feel unworthy of happiness. I felt my only choice was to accept the best available at that time, instead of demanding the best for *me*.

So, what have my relationship experiences taught me about myself?

I have learned that I can love, but there are no guarantees.

I have learned that I can love, but not be challenged.

I have learned that I can love, but not be truly compatible with the person I love.

I have learned that people change and evolve and being "all-in" may not necessarily be permanent.

I have learned that sometimes, despite the presence of love, stressful situations can simply be too much. Those difficulties create brand new issues, and they can exacerbate other seemingly insignificant problems. Some relationships are simply not strong enough to withstand stress tests.

I have learned that giving too much of myself, sacrificing more than I am willing, being out of my comfort zone, breeds resentment. That resentment can fester.

I have learned that I can love, but circumstances around us change. Those changes can be too challenging to overcome.

I know that I must try not to make people pay for mistakes others have made.

I have learned that keeping score is a dangerous idea. It erodes respect.

I have learned that I can love, but that I may not always be loved in return.

I have learned that I'm fearful of trusting too much, relying too much on another person.

What my experiences have shown me is how fundamental and critical it is to develop a strong sense of self. Life circumstances have made me recognize that I am my only constant companion, and my time is a precious commodity. How I choose to spend that time, and with whom, is significant. I must choose love carefully and I owe it to myself to not always simply accept any love that chooses me.

Several years ago, a friend set me up on a blind date at a party. My date didn't expect to arrive until later in the evening. I arrived early, consumed several drinks, and was not interested in him when he finally did arrive. But he asked me to go out for a dinner date three days later, and since I had just read Mark Manson's essay entitled "Fuck Yes," I agreed.

That decision turned out to be an excellent one: six-plus years later, we are still committed and truly enjoy each other's company. He is a constant source of support and a thoughtful partner. I very much cherish his companionship, and although our situation is somewhat unconventional—we maintain separate residences, don't co-parent, and don't share finances—it works for us.

Because I have learned to value myself differently, and I have proven that not only am I capable of being alone, but that I often enjoy it, I demand more. I will no longer find myself settling for the "best available."

Egg Baskets

I am a believer in fostering many friendships. When girls (more so than boys, it seems) are young, many long for belonging and the security of having a best-friend-forever relationship. They place a great deal of significance on having a well-publicized friendship like this. They proudly sign their birthday cards and yearbooks with the BFF acronym. They are dismayed and hurt deeply when that coveted BFF relationship dissolves and their former BFF is now using that term of endearment to describe someone else.

Friendship can be the source of much drama, much angst, and a great deal of behavioural analysis. One poorly worded attempt at explaining my feelings on this topic has provided a great deal of laughter for my daughter and myself. After a particularly tough pre-teen friendship situation unfolded, my daughter found herself feeling very alone and very vulnerable. Naturally, I was hurting for her too, and in my attempt to offer some advice, I ended up awkwardly and rather humorously advising her, "Try not to put all your egg friends in one egg basket."

Okay, I recognize now, and I recognized the moment it came out, that it was a word fail, but I stand by the message I was trying to convey. That message is to work hard at fostering friendships with many people. If you're fortunate to have a BFF, excellent! But have friends from the neighbourhood, friends from activities, friends from sports. Welcome friendships with people from other grades, other classes, other schools, other walks of life. Put yourself out there to expand your horizons. The reality is that you will forever face situations where you feel like, or you actually are, the only person without a partner. Science fair. Gym class. Prom date. Divorcee. Those tough situations are best handled when you have many sources from which to draw upon. If the only person you ever pair up with is the *only* person you have to rely upon, the pain of occasionally, or even permanently, not having *that* person available can be significant, even unbearable.

A single best friend may not always or "forever" hold that status. Sometimes that's *our* choice; sometimes it isn't. The best way to cope with that possible status change is to expand your friendship circles to ensure you don't place all your egg friends in one egg basket. Broaden your social network so that a single person doesn't bear all the friendship pressure.

I am now finding myself in a situation where I must heed the advice I have long been giving my children. Because I grew up in a large family and I am outgoing, my social life was always easy. When I joined the RCMP, I had built-in friendships from work. When I became a mom, I met other parents because of kids' classes or activities. I never had to work hard to establish connections because they came effortlessly. However, now that I'm retired, and my children are older and more independent, connections with other people don't happen as easily, quickly, or naturally as they did in the past. I must take my own advice about actively seeking out and cultivating new relationships.

It's time to think about *my* egg baskets.

Spiders, Slugs, and Bird Corpses

In July 2013, I was anxiously awaiting the arrival of Lorelei and her family. They were coming to stay with us for two nights, and the kids and I were excited to be hosting because we rarely have guests. The fridge and pantry were stocked, and we had lots of activities on our schedule.

The day before our guests' arrival, my teenaged neighbour came to play with the kids while I went to the gym in the morning. When I returned all sweaty, I figured that was as good a time as any to power-wash the back deck and the trampoline. Our house backs onto a forested area, so critters are problematic, and the backyard and deck are constantly covered with debris from the overgrown brush and tall trees. I always dread cleaning that grossness.

The kids and I went out to the back deck to assess what needed to be done so that the trampoline was usable. We were saddened to see that a large robin had lost its battle against one of the nine large windows. The corpse was a few days old and was positioned awkwardly on the ground below the deck. Disgusted and already disheartened with the work which lay ahead, I corralled the kids back inside, trying to distract them from the disgusting mess. I went to the garage, grabbed my shovel, and proceeded to pick up the bird's floppy body and fire it as far as I could it over the fence into the greenspace behind our house.

I then laboriously struggled to get the heavy power washer up the few steps to the deck. I was already overwhelmed and weary thinking about how long the cleaning would take. But my friends were arriving soon, and the job had to be done. With a big sigh, I set down the power washer so I could shift the patio furniture for effective cleaning. As I slid the stack of patio chairs, another robin, which had been dead longer than the first, unceremoniously plopped from the stack of chairs onto the deck. Frustrated, and even more grossed out, I positioned his limp, but not yet maggoty body, up and onto the shovel and proceeded to fling him over the fence as well. I used a broom to bat down the countless cobwebs, demolishing every one. I aggressively killed the never-ending parade of spiders. Suddenly angry, I looked at the patio furniture that was twelve years old—the same patio furniture that was a great fit for our previous deck, but a poor fit for our current one. With a fresh burst of energy and determination to purge, I began the very loud process of moving five of the six chairs, plus cushions, and one of the two stools, along with the umbrella and umbrella base, down the narrow sidewalk beside the house, ultimately to end up at the side of the road. Everything suddenly needed to be gone, except for a single chair that would allow me to be a one-mom audience for any upcoming trampoline performances.

Since a river is nearby, slugs around my home are enormous and come in a variety of vile colours, so I conducted a thorough slug check and disposed of any I could find. I then cleaned the trampoline with dish soap, sudsing it up with water from the hose and carefully rinsing it. A million choice curse words ran through my head, over and over.

Eyes filled with tears, I returned to the deck to find my two wide-eyed children with the deck door open, asking me if they could help. A tear slid down my cheek, and I reassured them that I appreciated their offer, but that it was heavy work, and I would come inside just as soon as I could.

When I was finally done, I was in tremendous pain, and my back was on fire. I was drenched with sweat and hose water, and cobwebs were stuck to me. The heaviness of running an entire house on my own seemed like way too much to bear. I was filthy and I still had to lug the heavy power washer back around to the front and into the garage.

Exhausted from exertion, and overwhelmed by nasty dead birds and slugs and spiders, I finally came in through the garage door. Rachel and Brett were waiting for me at the entrance to the laundry room and told me they had a surprise for me. Not wanting to bring my muddy, cobwebby outdoor clothes into the house, I took them off. The kids instructed me to close my eyes, then, each taking one of my hands they led me, clad only in my sweaty sports bra and underwear, into the kitchen.

Once there, I was told in two very excited voices that I could open my eyes. To my amazement, there was my lunch in front of me: a Babybel cheese, yogurt, a granola bar, some carrots. More importantly, there was a glass of my favourite wine (Latitude 50 white, from Gray Monk). It was noon! Beside the wine was a Crown Royal shot glass, also filled with wine; it was the "sampler," a tactic my son has employed from time to time to ensure that the bigger glass of wine is to my satisfaction!

Overcome, I couldn't stop thanking them. Despite my sweaty almost-naked self, I couldn't stop hugging them. But there was more. They proudly told me to turn around and look at the living room. Our living room *always* had a million action figures in and around the very large toy castle on the carpet. But that day, those action figures were *all* tidied up and put away. In awe, I thanked them again.

There was still more. I was ordered to close my eyes again while they led me up the stairs to my bedroom. When we arrived, two little voices excitedly told me to open my eyes. There on my white carpet was an outfit they had chosen for me for the day. The dress they had chosen was displayed beautifully, complete with jewelry accessories. To top it all off, the shower was running, and water was hot!

It was beautiful.

To recap:
Lunch made, accompanied by an apologetic, "Sorry, we can't cook."
Toys tidied.
Warm shower.
Clothes and pretty accessories carefully selected.

Wow.

What my children reminded me of that day was that although they wanted to help, they really couldn't have been of much assistance in the outside tasks. They understood how physically demanding those jobs were, so they came up with several creatively meaningful indoor gestures. They reminded me that regardless of the situation, there are many, many simple ways of demonstrating sympathy and empathy.

Recognize your limitations but know that those limitations don't render you completely helpless. There is something very powerful, exciting and gratifying about validating another person's emotions, so never stop contributing in whatever way is possible *for you*.

Part 5 –

Speaking Up

A Van Down by the River

Many years ago, one of my favourite segments on *Saturday Night Live* was Chris Farley as Matt Foley, the motivational speaker, who lived in a "van down by the river." It was, and still is, hilarious; for me, it never gets old.

Shortly after I returned to work in Kitimat, I was asked to present at a women's wellness seminar in Kitimat. Since I was newly back in the community post-rehab, I was humbled and flattered to receive the request. While research states that glossophobia, the fear of public speaking, affects up to seventy-five percent of the population, given my background with teaching, instructing, and coaching, I was somewhat comfortable speaking to groups. Many people tremble even thinking about speaking in public, but I was excited for the opportunity.

As I prepared for my presentation, I began to feel a bit nervous. I was proud of my accomplishments over the previous year but unsure of which highlights, or how much of my story, to share with the participants, so I gave the content a great deal of consideration.

The day of the seminar, I stewed about what to wear and tried on several different outfits before making a final decision. I was quite pleased with myself for having a "high heel" prosthetic leg, one that I could wear with dress shoes, and of course, after my absence from the community for rehabilitation, I wanted to impress everyone with how well I had recovered. Wearing my high heel leg was certainly going to wow 'em all!

I painstakingly selected my clothing and my shoes, opting for business casual even though those in attendance would have better recognized me in my police uniform or sweatpants. I carefully applied my makeup, and I allowed my hair to be big and wavy, not tied back in a work-like bun. I looked myself in the mirror, gave myself a mental pep talk, and adjusted my posture. I walked, inwardly nervously and outwardly confidently, into the venue and into the interested stares of many local women. In front of the crowd, I slowly eased into my speech. I detailed my shooting, my ten months of hard work, some of the challenges I had faced, and ultimately my successes.

When I'd finished my presentation, I opened the floor up for questions and I quickly realized that, by the nature of the questions being asked, the attendees were mostly curious. It became apparent that although my story resonated, they really needed a visual to make it believable. They wanted to see, with their own eyes, my prosthetic leg and equipment. Suddenly I found myself with my carefully selected dress pants rolled up to my thigh so I could show the women in attendance what my artificial leg looked like. Many of those women in the audience had known me pre-shooting, and they'd had difficulty wrapping their heads around the fact that I was now an amputee. Standing there, apparently two-legged, with no limp, didn't compute. They needed verification that the struggles I just detailed had in fact taken place. Maybe it just didn't seem real?

I had worried about dressing and appearing "normal," when what was truly of interest to the audience was observing first-hand what made me *different*. I realized that, like children, adults need to satisfy their curiosity by seeing my leg, my disability, with their own eyes. Telling them about it was simply not enough.

Even though it had unfolded differently than I'd expected, my presentation was very well-received that day, and it was so rewarding! At the end, I rolled my pantleg back down, stood up, straightened my shirt, and felt so inspiring, so confident, so proud.

That day was a turning point for me in many ways, not the least of which was that I became a motivational speaker; nothing like the legendary Matt Foley, but a motivational speaker nonetheless!

That initial post-amputation presentation was quickly followed by several other eye-opening experiences.

After I explained to a curious ten-year-old what happened to my leg, he looked at me inquisitively and said, "Did you get dead?" Confused and caught off-guard, I said, "Uh, no." That was it.

I was sitting on a couch visiting friends, and their young son was on the floor beside my artificial leg. The boy's Transformers and superhero toys were strewn about the family room all around us, and while the adults chatted, I noticed the boy looking around. He would look at me, then down at my leg, then towards his toys. Finally, after several cycles of looking at me and then at his toys, it was as if a lightbulb had gone off. He exclaimed, "You're a robot!" That was it.

Upon the first time seeing me after my amputation, another friend's young son looked me up and down. He looked at the pole of my prosthetic leg then at my sound left leg and back again. He nodded knowingly and observed, "Your skin is right off, and your bones are silver." That was it.

One time in a YMCA change room, I was putting on my royal blue rubber shower sock. The sock is wider at the foot, narrower at the top where it fits against my thigh, and I step into that sock with my prosthetic to prevent my equipment from getting wet. A little girl looked at my bright blue sock, then up at my long, frizzy red hair, and back to my sock. Curiously, she asked me what the sock was for. I told her I use it for swimming. Her eyes became wide, she looked back at my hair, and announced excitedly, "You're a mermaid!" Laughing, her mom told me that her daughter's favourite Disney movie was *The Little Mermaid*, and she thought I was just like Ariel, the red-headed main character. That was it.

Those early moments reinforced to me that adults are simply children with better filters, more-evolved social training. Adults have the same curiosity but are reluctant to succumb to their instincts. I became acutely aware that people need visuals to believe, and often, quite simple, direct explanations suffice.

Even more importantly, I realized that once people are past the brief shock, surprise, intrigue, our individual differences matter a whole lot less, sometimes not at all. Much of the time those differences are irrelevant.

Over the years I have given dozens of presentations, all around the country. My messaging varies only slightly, depending on the audience. And because of that initial speech in Kitimat, I often wear shorts and *always* do a show-and-tell component. I have even been known to occasionally throw in a cartwheel (although those are few and far between now)!

I have been questioned numerous times as to why I choose to speak publicly about my shooting, my most personal experiences. Family members, friends and co-workers alike stare at me, incredulous, wondering why on earth I would want to put myself through the stress of recounting my shooting, my trauma. Why, when so many are fearful of public speaking, would I want to relive, in front of an audience, the worst day in my life?

Quite simply, I must.

Some people cry, some nod. Some laugh, some smile nervously. Some stick around to talk afterwards. Some prefer to email me and share their feedback privately. I cherish every single response, every reaction, every emotion, because I believe and hope that my words resonate on some level with every individual in the audience. I feel that because I face that universal fear of speaking in public and I do that by sharing my most intimate moments, I invite compassion and lend credibility to the struggles, visible or not, that challenge others. Because I'm able do this, because I'm willing to share, to be vulnerable, I continue to speak. Our world needs more compassion, more understanding, more openness, more transparency.

And luckily, there have been many rewards for me along the way. I've travelled to New Brunswick, where I met some fabulously warm-hearted East-Coasters, and participated in a very entertaining dinner theatre comedy improv show.

I've travelled to the Yukon to speak to children and fellow RCMP members. There, I went quadding across the most beautiful northern terrain, and had the good fortune of going dogsledding.

I travelled to Ottawa to speak at the prestigious

The Yukon.

National Press Club, and while the kind of audience was unfamiliar, it was very rewarding.

I travelled to Nova Scotia to speak at a Women in Policing conference. I left feeling empowered and with a newfound sense of comradeship.

Every time I speak, I share the triumphs and the joy I've experienced during my journey. But I can't be true to myself if I omit talking of my personal struggle with PTSD. While I've been criticized for sharing the depth of my pain on my darkest days, I wouldn't be being honest if I didn't do that. I recognize that revealing my vulnerability may make others feel uncomfortable, but I also know that if I don't describe how low my valleys have been, if I don't share the pain and the suffering, the peaks and triumphs are not nearly as meaningful.

For example, I know for a fact that when I agreed to speak at a work conference, a supervisor in the RCMP said afterwards, "She's just fucked." That was a very odd comment, given that the speaker preceding me was a male colleague who had detailed his own darkest PTSD struggles. His story was raw, painful, emotional, and hit many of the same chords as my own. Yet for one member of the audience, the male speaker was tough and brave. Me? I was "just fucked."

That remark stung ... a lot. Baring my heart and soul in front of strangers is difficult enough, but doing it in front of colleagues, people who may have had direct involvement in my career, was downright intimidating. I became preoccupied with who had made the comment, and why. I also became acutely aware that letting my guard down, opening myself up, showing vulnerability, opened the door for others to judge, to attack. It was devastating because I assumed that my audience was full of sympathetic, kindred-spirited fellow police officers who would applaud my courage. Instead, I couldn't believe how another could dare criticize me! Didn't people even have a basic respect for the fact that I willingly shared my personal, most private pain, simply so they could learn and grow as managers, as supervisors, as police officers ... as human beings? Didn't that, in and of itself, warrant some level of respect?

I had to process that hurt and if I'm honest, I can still get riled up about that one member's insensitivity. But I have come to realize that it was exactly that—*one* person's perspective. Maybe I touched a nerve with that member. I don't know and I can't let myself care. I shared what I believed was valuable. I wanted to help the men and women in the organization understand what I went through. I wanted to highlight gaps, increase awareness, promote change.

The numerous positive comments and emails I received after that speech far outweighed the one negative comment. I was "relatable" and "open" and "frank" and "funny" and "well-spoken." That feedback was proof that I was far from "fucked"!

I remind myself that sharing my experiences publicly is a choice, *my* choice. I still believe that my ability to speak, to show humanity, to be vulnerable, to talk about my deepest and darkest moments, to share my loss, my grief, helps others. People will judge, but maybe they'll begin to be less judgmental after having listened. Maybe I'll help someone learn compassion. Maybe I'll help someone build resilience. Maybe I'll help someone realize it is okay to ask for help, admit that he/she isn't invincible. Maybe I'll help someone recognize that he or she isn't alone.

Maybe even more importantly, it helps me keep my personal challenges in perspective, and I selfishly admit that speaking is instrumental in helping me cope, too. Sharing can be both rewarding and therapeutic.

Shifting Perspectives

Years ago, while I was home in Ontario visiting my family, my mom announced that she had committed me to doing a speech at a local elementary school assembly. I was *very* annoyed and made no attempts to hide my frustration with her. Holiday time is limited, and my calendar in my hometown gets busy quickly. I did not want to be obliged to do a speech during my precious vacation time.

However, I dressed in my shorts and sneakers and headed off to the school gym for my presentation, throwing digs at my mom on the drive over for her lack of consultation with me.

The presentation went well, and I concluded with the customary show and tell, as well as a cartwheel for effect. Afterwards, I was chatting with administrative staff while most of the students dispersed. As the crowd thinned, I noticed a special education assistant lingering nearby, eyes darting from me to her student. She and I made eye contact, and then she approached me to explain that her student was anxiously awaiting an opportunity to speak with me. I saw that the young girl was about ten years old and had a physical disability requiring her to wear a cumbersome leg brace, which kept her legs apart at what looked to be an uncomfortable distance. That brace contraption was accompanied by crutches, and as a result, her mobility was severely compromised. I greeted the little girl and enthusiastically answered all her questions. She seemed incredulous about the fact that part of my leg was missing. When her assistant noticed the girl's bus waiting outside, she thanked me and told the girl it was time to leave. As the young girl reluctantly turned to begin the slow trek towards the bus, she stopped and looked back at me one last time, eyes wide. She shook her head slowly and said, "I'm *so* glad I have *both* of my legs!"

I was speechless. And immediately tearful.

A little girl, with a physical disability far more limiting than mine, felt *fortunate* in comparison to me.

That experience, and her perspective, were incredible gifts, and I will never forget the depth of the emotion I felt about her observation.

Every person faces adversity: grief, loss, injury, illness, and death of a loved one. Suffering just manifests differently for everyone. I appreciate that *everyone* has a story; mine may just be a little more dramatic than some. While telling my story has been mostly positive, I also don't want to stay stuck in it, stuck in the past.

That school presentation, the one I was *angry* about having to do, was one of the most profound experiences of my life. That little girl taught me a powerful lesson. *Her* perspective forced *me* to think differently. It serves as an ongoing reminder to feel grateful—grateful for waking up, grateful for all the good I have in my life. When I am struggling to remain positive, I think of that little girl. I think about her outlook, how it clearly helped her cope, and how it changed me. Studies show that happy people are more likely to reach out to others, to take risks. Positive thinking evokes good feelings and improves relationships and personal health. Unhappy people, on the other hand, are more apt to be critical, self-conscious, negative. I prefer the first option.

I also know that truly valuing myself, and being honest with myself, means that sometimes I will have to *fight* to find that happiness and positivity. Those feelings aren't automatic and sometimes they don't last long. Most of the time those feelings are choices. And when the choices seem more difficult than usual, or when joy seems out of reach, we must make an *effort* to get it all back. We owe that to ourselves.

I'm convinced that trying to maintain perspective and choosing to have a positive attitude has a ripple effect. It improves my own wellness and dramatically improves the quality of life for myself, my children, and everyone with whom we come into contact.

I want my perspective to be *just* like that ten-year-old girl's.

Do Legs Grow Back?

My brother, Steve, a Grade 7 teacher, often ropes me into speaking to his class when I'm in my hometown on holidays. I know he's happy to provide his students a change of pace by utilizing me and my holiday-induced freed-up schedule, and truthfully, I always end up enjoying myself. One of these times, after I shared my story with his class, I offered a Q & A period.

"Constable White, is your leg ever going to grow back?"

This question, understandably, threw me off. Way off. I had given many speeches and had incorporated into my main presentation most of the questions that seemed to arise. But this … this was unexpected!

Racking my brain (while the entire class is snickering and my brother ducks out of the back of the classroom to hide his facial expression), I come up with, "Well, I know some animals have the ability to grow body parts back and I wish I were one of them. But unfortunately, no, it isn't going to grow back."

The giggling quickly simmered down while the students digested this statement, trying to determine if it was fact. I seized the opportunity to move on and quickly answered the rest of the questions.

Frankly, I thought I handled that awkward situation well. The rest of the kids probably wouldn't have let their classmate live it down for asking such a ridiculous question (after all, they were twelve), so the fact that I readily had a comeback, which almost somewhat legitimized the silliness, was a win. I was fortunate in that moment to be able to think quickly on my feet and thwart the ridicule so the student didn't feel foolish.

I learned from that day. I learned that, try as I might, I cannot predict what is going to come out of another human's mouth and I cannot predict other people's behaviour. I also learned that being prepared takes concentration, flexibility, respect. It also requires quick-thinking and a sense of humour.

A Slap on the Ass

When I was a substitute teacher, I was assigned a thirty-student Grade 9 English class, which included only three girls. I tried to keep the class quiet, but it was difficult to do for seventy-five minutes as I had been left no instructions.

When the end-of-class bell finally rang, the boy who had shown within seconds of class starting that he was the class clown was the last one out the door. As I switched off the light with a sigh of relief that class was over, I was startled by a swift slap on my ass! I turned around and the boy looked at me with a goofy smile, almost taunting me, then tore off down the hall. In that moment, as a fit, shocked, and then angry, twenty-one-year-old university phys ed student, I made the impulsive decision to race after him.

I chased him, caught him, grabbed his shirt, and threw him up against the lockers. Breathing heavily after the exertion, I stared furiously into his eyes, appalled at the disrespect he had shown me by slapping my ass. He was about my size, but he was caught off-guard and clearly a little fearful. I chastised him and let him go, shaking my head as I walked away.

In the moment, I had reacted hastily without considering consequences of the fact that I, as the teacher in authority, did not exactly handle the situation in a professional manner.

Later, when facing employment issues with the RCMP, I thought often about that slap on the ass.

Like all Mounties, throughout my career, I volunteered, or was "volun-told," to participate in various community events. Among other things, I have dressed up as Safety Bear, I have participated in many committees, and I have been stationed at mall kiosks.

Me as Safety Bear!

Community Policing at the mall.

When I was doing a fair amount of public speaking, I was approached by a speaker's agency about representation, but I had declined. Since I had made an agreement with management that my speaking engagements would not interfere with my day-to-day job responsibilities, it made sense for me coordinate my engagements independently.

One day I learned via email that I had been scheduled to speak at a large policing function. The presentation had already been approved by management, but it was the first I had heard of it.

Looking for more information, I followed up and was told that because the cause was a good one, I would be permitted to use work time to give the speech as part of my policing duties. However, that was contradictory to our agreement. Since I had been invited to speak at three other functions, but hadn't yet committed, I suggested a compromise. If I agreed to speak at the policing event as part of my duties, could consideration be given to the other community-based requests?

I was advised that I could use on-duty time for the policing event, but not for the others. Those would have to be done, as per our original agreement, on my own time. This was unlike Safety Bear performances or community policing at a mall kiosk, and I declined to do the policing speech as part of my duties.

After much negotiation, I presented at that policing function (as well as the other three events). But since my shooting is an intensely personal experience, when and where I choose to share that experience will be *my* decision. That principle is incredibly important to me, and I only agreed to do those presentations after reaching mutually agreeable terms for all.

The slap on the ass and the speaking issue both highlight an important principle: carefully choosing my battles is critical.

When responding, or weighing whether to engage in potential conflict, what are the physical, emotional, psychological, and financial costs?

That then translates into:

- What is my desired end state? What's my goal?
- Is it a power struggle?
- Is it money, reimbursement, recognition, an award?
- Is it time?

- Is it an apology?

- Am I simply fighting to win? To be viewed as "being right"?

- What outcome is acceptable? If I don't, or can't, identify to myself what I am trying to accomplish from the outset, then there will be no sense of closure when I finally reach that place.

And in getting there, the questions are more about personal cost and sacrifice:

- How much am I willing to devote to this battle?

- Will this battle cost me my health? My well-being?

- Will this battle affect my psychological state?

- Will it negatively impact my relationships? My family? Friends? Employment?

- If there is money involved, what's the limit? Will I promise myself that once I reach that cap, regardless of the outcome or which stage I'm at, I will cease the battle?

- What outcome can I reasonably expect? What can I *accept*? What can I live with?

I try to analyze every challenge now, personal or professional, through this kind of a lens. If I pursue the challenge, I remind myself to review my motives regularly and carefully. I focus on the core issues: why I'm fighting, and what outcome I might reasonably expect. I have also learned to set frequent deadlines at varying intervals in the process so that I can check in with myself, re-evaluate next steps, and change strategies if necessary.

The power of conviction is strong, but careful consideration must be given to choices I make and how I react to external pressures. My choices may be contrary to what others believe I should do, or what they think *they* would do if they were faced with a similar situation. I also recognize, however, that doing nothing, or simply remaining silent, may be even more damaging or stressful than doing what *I* believe is right for *me*.

Responses can be spontaneous and impulsive (like the classroom reaction), or they can be strategic and calculated (like the speaking matter). I'm trying to remember to choose wisely because there are many ways to react to a slap on the ass.

Part 6 –

Stepping Away

Lopsided Loyalties

Years ago, my children had an opportunity to participate in a mini-Mountie camp. They loved the experience, but what surprised me most was how *I* was the one bursting with pride at night when they regaled me with stories of their day, one-upping and interrupting each other, competing with each other to share their excitement with me. They told me about all they had learned, the instructors they admired. They demonstrated their newly acquired self-defence skills, much the same way I had done for my family when I was in Depot. I became all misty-eyed when, on the final day of camp, my two beaming kids marched around the gymnasium performing their "graduation" drill display in their matching T-shirts and caps. I was emotional that day as I listened to the commanding sounds of the bagpiper playing the familiar music that represented so much to me.

I joined the RCMP knowing that there is a bond, a unique brother/sister-hood that is a critical part of the first responder world. It may seem odd to those in other professions, but in policing, we devote ourselves to public service, we make sacrifices, and I believe we have expectations about what we deserve in return. I believed that loyalty and pride were mutual. Policing, after all, is more than a profession; it isn't just a job to most of us. It is a lifestyle.

However, what I recognized long ago is that my relationship with the RCMP was not in fact reciprocal. I had committed, I was "all in," and I wanted desperately to feel a level of reciprocation. However, for the most part, I just didn't.

I liken this to a one-sided romantic relationship, the kind where one person is crazy about the other, but the same level of emotion is simply not returned. It was like many domestic situations I handled on general duty. The kind where one person will give up almost anything, including self-worth, simply to please her partner. The kind where one person would go to almost any lengths to prove his worthiness. The kind where one person thinks that if she could simply talk to her partner face to face, look into his eyes, she could convince the person to love her equally and unconditionally. The kind where he is certain that, given time, he will persuade her to feel the same way.

That analogy became an accurate representation of my relationship with the Force. I recognized that it was lopsided, a one-way street. I also realized that the expectation I had held was silly; the RCMP is an entity, an enormous, evolving organization comprising thousands of people. It simply cannot be compared to a relationship with a person, and I had been naïve to think of it as such.

In 2017, I had the opportunity to speak at Depot at a training course for the newly established Disability Management Program. I hadn't been at Depot in years, but the training course was of great personal interest so, although I wasn't exactly thrilled to be flying to cold, snowy Regina in February, I did.

The challenge I faced, however, was that at the time, I was off work on medical leave. I had taken several devastating falls, and my pain issues were not well managed. My physical deterioration was taking a huge toll on me, and my PTSD was exacerbated because of the frustration with my body. To boot, I was in constant fear of opening my inbox to find a message advising me that, due to my inability to work, a medical discharge from the RCMP would soon be forthcoming. I was stressed and overwhelmed with my personal circumstances, but I felt compelled to offer my insight to course participants. Since I had been lobbying for internal policy change, I felt this would be an excellent opportunity to share my experiences and possibly help make a difference for the RCMP membership at large.

When I arrived in Regina, I felt almost instantly overcome with nostalgia. It was a cold, brisk, sunny day. It was lightly snowing. And I was unexpectedly emotional.

I wandered the grounds at Depot, checking out the new heritage centre and the mess hall.

I wandered the canteen (store), noting the boot-polishing and gun-cleaning supplies I had once required daily. I looked closely at the badge cases and recalled how much thought had gone into choosing the exact model for my own when I received it. I sifted through the countless mugs and T-shirts and other paraphernalia bearing RCMP logos; these were the items I had excitedly purchased for family members when I was a young, proud cadet in 1995.

I smiled and reminisced about Troop 12 as I watched new cadets in ugly, brown, Force-issued pants jogging double-time on the roads around base, fists to chests. They hadn't yet earned the right to wear their real uniforms, their "blues."

I quietly entered the drill hall and watched, with misty eyes, a troop nearing graduation, practise their marching manoeuvres. I was mesmerized and transported back in time to that day in 1996 when I, too, had marched proudly in sync with my troopmates in that very gym.

I spent some time at the fallen officers' memorial, paying tribute to my comrades who have died in the line of duty. I was weepy and contemplative, introspective while acknowledging the ultimate sacrifice those brave men and women had made. I silently thanked them and their families for their courage. Overcome with survivor's guilt, all I could think was, "but for the grace of God go I."

But what struck me most was the overwhelming sense of pride that I felt when I was there, despite the years that had passed.

Surprisingly, simply being there on base represented so very much to me. It represented my first real, solid attempt at "adulting." It represented independence, humility, personal growth, commitment, perseverance. It represented hard work and teamwork. It represented loyalty and unification.

I felt as if I had come full circle, and a tremendous sense of peace washed over me. It was time to embrace that, like all life experiences, my policing career was an incredible phase of my life and had certainly helped shape me, but it no longer defined me.

I knew then and there, that when it was time for me to leave the Force, time to close that chapter, I would no longer consider it to be "losing" part of myself.

Pedophiles and Porn

"What happened to the guy who shot you?"

People are either awkward and stutter before they ask, or they blurt it out suddenly and instantly feel embarrassed that they asked it. Regardless, the curiosity is always there. I get that.

The simple answer is that after he shot me, there was a ten-hour stand-off, and ultimately, he was found dead inside his residence. He died as a result of a self-inflicted gunshot wound.

I feel sorry for his family members, but the truth of the matter is, there is a selfish part of me that's relieved I didn't have to face a court case. I did have to sit through an extremely emotional coroner's inquest, so I couldn't imagine having to sit through days of court proceedings. I also couldn't imagine having to come to terms with whatever the outcome of a court case may have been. I suspect that, because the situation was so personal, no outcome would have seemed satisfactory or fair.

The man who shot me almost murdered me. He died not knowing that he hadn't.

The man who shot me almost murdered both of my partners.

The man who shot me fired two bullets. One came terrifyingly close to killing my partner. The other narrowly missed my other partner and struck me. We three are left to process the facts, the realities, the damage that it caused all of us, physically and psychologically. Forever. I am grateful for their heroic actions, but I am also certain that their lives were permanently changed that day too.

That gunman was an alleged pedophile. He was being investigated for possession of child porn. He became an attempted murderer. To me, he was a bad guy.

I recall a comment I had heard from a former military colleague. His perspective was that when military personnel go on deployment, they know exactly who their enemy is. When they return from deployment, they feel safe from those enemy forces.

However, he expressed how challenging he considered police work to be because the enemy wasn't clearly identified groups of people in foreign countries; enemies of a police officer could easily be a neighbour, an acquaintance, a stranger. That enemy could be virtually anyone on Canadian soil.

For me, that was an intriguing observation. I so admire and respect our military members, even more so since having been given an opportunity to work alongside some of them as part of the Vancouver 2010 Integrated Security Unit for the Olympic and Paralympic Games. Their commitment to, and sacrifices for, Canadians is unparalleled.

Because of what happened to me so early in my career, it isn't surprising that I had quickly begun to believe that *everyone* is a bad guy. Before policing, I thought most people were inherently good and I embarked upon my profession naively. But I quickly realized that although some, or as I like to believe, *most* people certainly appreciate law enforcement, there are many who don't.

Thankfully, despite what happened to me, I have slowly shifted my perspective back to its positive pre-"getting shot" state. Everyone is *not* a bad guy or an enemy—in fact, quite the contrary. There are kind, hopeful, compassionate, inspiring people everywhere. I'm so very fortunate that while it has been a process to arrive in this place, the number of good guys *far* outweighs the bad.

Armchair Quarterbacks

The overwhelming majority of our thousands of RCMP members are solid, respected role models. Our members are truly our most valuable asset, and I wholeheartedly believe that we must treat them as such.

Police officers protect others—it is our job description—and we risk our lives, over and over, to do so. People in the general public expect this of us, and they take it for granted. Yet many of those very same people in the public most certainly would never willingly do the same. They couldn't or wouldn't pass the training, put the uniform on, and bravely run toward and into unpredictable, often dangerous situations. Police officers are expected to make sound, split-second decisions, and the expectation is that those decisions will *always* be the right ones. Those decisions, often made in highly stressful situations, are then scrutinized, judged, and criticized, both in the moment and for long periods of time afterwards, especially in our era of video recordings. Those decisions are questioned from an internal protocol standpoint, and they're questioned publicly via the media and during judicial proceedings. The public, however, fails to remember that police officers must make those decisions in the midst of chaos and tragedy, often with frighteningly little information. Far too often, while doing our best to try to uphold the law and keep the peace, *we* are treated like the "bad guys," the enemies.

If a police-involved situation goes sideways or ends in tragedy, other police officers sometimes choose to cope with it by assuming that there *must* have been a mistake. The members involved must have made a poor judgment call and *deserved* the negative outcome. That message has surfaced several times, and it is unequivocally unfair. We are highly trained and, for the most part, we absolutely do the best we can in risky situations. But if things don't end well, it doesn't necessarily mean the member(s) involved did something wrong.

When I was shot, I don't believe anything could have changed the outcome. I have long been at peace with the events of that day and how my tragedy unfolded. However, I have heard, on several occasions, judgments from others who weren't there, which indicated that tactical mistakes or human error *had* to have factored in, otherwise the result wouldn't have been tragic injury. I disagree. Negative outcomes are not always the result of preventable human error. Things don't always add up. There is no reliable mathematical equation that can fully account for human behaviour and split-second decision-making.

I have also heard more than once that what happened to me would not have happened to a man. Seriously! But sadly, it has been said. In fact, I know I was called a "split tail" (a derogatory term for a female) and I was just another "dumb female" who made a mistake and deserved what I got.

Unfortunately, I am confident these types of misogynistic beliefs were and are held even more commonly than I care to admit. Blaming my shooting on my gender is not only insulting; it is downright ludicrous. If that argument somehow makes another person feel invincible, that I must have made a fundamentally *female* mistake and ultimately deserved what I got, it is a sad and dangerously flawed coping strategy.

This action + this equipment + this knowledge + this gender + this training simply must = positive, desired outcome.

Not every situation can be easily, quickly, efficiently, and smoothly handled. Life simply doesn't work like this, and we are naïve, only fooling ourselves, if we believe that every single negative situation can be prevented. Police plan and strategize and hypothesize and prepare to the best of our collective abilities, but sometimes shit happens. It just does, and there are many, many factors that come into play.

No one is invincible. You are only fooling yourself if you think bad things could never happen to you because you're smarter, wiser, or better equipped. Or simply because you're male. It may all in fact be true, but bad things may still happen. It may not be true, and bad things may still happen.

Try to avoid being an "armchair quarterback." Try not to justify or rationalize all the things you would have done differently. You truly have no idea what you would have done differently—or the same. You may think you know but you have the luxury of time and distance and different information. If you weren't there, you simply don't know. As difficult as it is to accept that there are uncontrollable situational and environmental factors, varying individual factors, there is no guarantee that your outcome would have been any different or better than mine was. It may well not have.

I encourage everyone to do their research and try not to jump to conclusions. Don't allow narrow-minded, biased, media reports to dictate your opinions. Know that what is presented publicly is a small slice of reality.

I urge you to be respectful, be fair, be just. I encourage you to refrain from judgments. Remind yourself of the risks that police and all first responders and soldiers take. There are thousands of them out there every single day, quietly putting their lives on the line, doing their damnedest to keep people safe.

For me.

For you.

For all Canadians.

Shoelaces

One evening we were dispatched to a call for a suicidal male. We rushed to the scene to find an intoxicated man unconscious on the floor of his townhouse with shoelaces wrapped around his neck. It was clear from the scene, and what we had been told, that his intention had been to hang himself. He had tried but was unsuccessful. We cut the laces to alleviate the pressure it was still putting on his neck, and he slowly regained consciousness as paramedics arrived. Gradually, he was able to function, albeit drunkenly. We assured him he was going to be looked after, but it was clear he needed a mental health assessment, so after a little persuasion he agreed to accompany us to the hospital. He was disoriented but as he began to come around more, he attempted to flirt with me as he walked in his stocking feet up the stairs to the front door.

When we arrived at the front door of the house, I held his jacket out for him and instructed him to put on his shoes before going outside. He looked at the shoes, and slowly, in his inebriated state, it registered that his sneakers no longer had laces in them. His demeanour changed instantly, and angrily, he began ranting, cursing me, blaming *me* for having cut his shoelaces, the very ones that he himself had wrapped around his neck in a drunken attempt to end his life.

I often think of this story because his reaction is in keeping with what many of us do. When something goes wrong, or we are wronged, instinctively we look outwardly to assign blame. We want to lash out, point fingers, accuse others of poor behaviour or damaging decisions. It seems much easier to criticize others as opposed to looking inwardly at what our own contributions have been.

I am thankful that attempted suicide incident did not have a tragic outcome and simply became a story about assigning blame. It became a personal reminder about making fair and unbiased assessments, about taking ownership for our decisions. It evolved into a lesson about acknowledging and accepting my own roles in my life, my decisions. It became a way to view life circumstances, not by what happens *to* me, but about what happens *because* of my choices. I learned to better analyze what my own contributions to my personal circumstances may be. It became about not always looking for external answers but looking inward for guidance, for that sought-after direction about how to change and move forward in positive ways.

It became about not blaming others for my own actions. It became about harsh realities and undeniable truths—and *not* blaming other people for wrecking my shoelaces.

Don't Sweat Raisins

When my daughter was three-years-old, she and her infant brother were strapped into their car seats while I drove to her much-loved gymnastics class. She and I were happily singing along to the catchy tunes playing on the *Backyardigans* DVD when she suddenly stopped singing and announced, "I have raisin in my nose."

Not sure what I heard, I turned the volume down, looked at her in the rearview mirror, and said, "What?"

She calmly looked out the window at the fields lining the rural road and said, "I have raisin in my nose."

And she promptly fell asleep.

Alarmed, my mind began to spin. There was nowhere to pull over so I had to drive a few kilometres up the road before I could find a safe spot. Hastily,

I exited the vehicle, ran around to her side, and opened the sliding door. She was sleeping soundly, but snoring uncharacteristically, and I looked up her nostrils. Something black was definitely blocking one of her nostrils. I tried to manoeuvre it down and out, but it was wedged up tightly.

I quickly jumped back in the driver's seat and turned the vehicle around while she continued snoring loudly. I was speeding to the medical clinic, worried that the raisin was dangerously obstructing her breathing. I was panicking and catastrophizing the entire ten-minute drive. When we arrived at the clinic, I parked crookedly, jumped out of the vehicle, woke her up, and collected her brother's car seat. We raced inside, and I couldn't get my words out fast enough.

The front desk staff was reassuring, and the doctor tended to us quickly. He assessed Rachel and confirmed that yes, in fact, there *was* a raisin quite far up her nose. Laughing as he produced a long, tweezer-type tool, he told me, "You'd be surprised at how many things kids jam up there!" He swiftly and expertly extracted the offending raisin while Rachel sat there completely unfazed, impatient to get to her gymnastics class.

I think of that raisin story often because I use it as a reminder to *try* not to overreact, to keep perspective. I recognize that I was a new mom, and instances like jamming a raisin up a nose and blocking breathing were new experiences, but it was far from the monumental disaster I had initially believed it to be. I use it to remind myself to be calmer, more patient. I use it to remind myself not to make a massive disaster out of a minor event.

Like the author Richard Carlson taught us, "Don't sweat the small stuff" ... or the raisins.

"F"

When I was a figure skater in my youth, I would spend hours on patch, scribing out my patterns, doing figure eights, perfecting the shapes, and fretting over double edges. Day after day I would work on perfecting my dance steps. During free skate sessions, I spun until snot flew out of my nose (it really happens) and body positions were just right. I visualized intricate dance footwork sequences, spins, and jumps, practising them in any open floor space. I dreamed about executing those moves flawlessly when it counted.

A few times a year, I would face a test day, and those days would represent the culmination of weeks of disciplined practice. The rink would be quiet, and stress levels were high. Ice usually seemed less than ideal—too hard and it cracked and crunched beneath my blades, or too soft so it felt too forgiving, too mushy. We would all fidget with our dresses, our tights, our gloves, our sweaters, our laces, trying to breathe, to stay warm and limber.

Passing meant I could move onwards and upwards. Failing meant that I had to spend countless more hours working on the same moves, same solos, listening to the same music, waiting patiently for the next test day, inevitably months down the road.

At long last, when my name was called for my turn, I would nervously skate to my designated starting spot on the ice, feeling as if all eyes were on me, though the audiences were always small. I would take a deep breath and wait for the music or the instruction to begin. I would perform my test, in the best way possible for me for that day, and then hit the dressing room, relieved to be done. Performance anxiety would then quickly be replaced with an almost palpable apprehension about results. I would pack up my skates, put them in the car, and wait, consumed with nervousness.

I would wait, sometimes for what seemed like an eternity, for the stern-looking head judge to emerge from the judges' room with the highly anticipated results. All eyes would be on the door of that room, and when it finally opened, skaters and parents and coaches would hustle over, desperate for a glimpse of the results sheet.

I would squint to find my name on the freshly posted results list, and my eyes would follow the line beside my name. There, I would see a letter indicating my result. That letter, written in large, bold printing would be a "P" or an "F." P = pass. F = fail. To me, it always seemed as if the "F's" were in bolder, larger font than the "P's," unquestionably to further humiliate those who received them. The results were always greeted with varying combinations of squeals of delight and tears of frustration.

More often than I care to admit or remember, I would see that letter "F" and bolt out to my mom's waiting car. There, demoralized and embarrassed, I would let loose and bawl the entire way home, wiping my nose and my tears, cursing. I would lament the injustice, the hours of hard work, the dedication, the perseverance, and wonder what, if anything, I could have done differently. I also would question my devotion to the sport that meant so much to me.

Through the pain and over time, I came to realize how much those test days taught me. They taught me how to reframe what constitutes true failure. Skating ignited a passion in me, a passion I couldn't replicate elsewhere. Those test days taught me about perseverance, commitment, dedication. They taught me about time management and setting goals, and those experiences, both positive and negative, were undoubtedly character-building.

If I had chosen to leave the RCMP after having lost my leg, I know now that I would not have considered that a failure. I know how much time, energy, perseverance, and sacrifice I made. I also know how much wisdom, confidence, and independence I gained because of the hurdles I had to overcome. Continuing to work for the RCMP was a difficult decision, and one I didn't make lightly, but had I chosen a different path, I most certainly would not have viewed that decision to leave as a personal failure.

When I returned to work in 1999, desperate to regain and resume my former life, that included my boyfriend. He was also posted to the same detachment, and although our relationship prior to my shooting had been rocky, and we were seeing other people when I was shot, we rekindled our romance. We had some disruptions, but married in 2002, and had our children in 2003 and 2005; however, relocations, work, medical issues, and various other stressors were driving a wedge between us, and things were becoming unpleasant. But I made a deal with myself; I would do what I felt *I* could to salvage our situation. When I arrived at a place where I felt I had done what was within *my* power, the painfully obvious conclusion was divorce. I gave myself permission to let go, to take what was, in my Catholic world, an unconventional path: divorce.

My coveted "white picket fence" scenario was brief, or maybe in the truest sense, it never really was at all; however, it was no failure. Naturally, I questioned it, and the whys, and the hows, and certainly I wondered what might have been had certain things not happened—that's normal. But my marriage gave me the gift of tremendous personal growth as a woman, and an opportunity to be a mom to two incredible human beings. That phase of my life also showed me so many things: strength, the power of conviction, the importance of independence, the importance of learning self-love.

So, when my marriage ended, I never considered it to be an "F." Others may have, but I did not.

When I think about the time in 2004 that I had to accept that I could no longer be an operational police officer and could not continue with the pace of a shift worker, I no longer view it as a failure. It represents a shift in thinking. Now, I am able to view that time as a way of facing reality, a chance to reprioritize, an opportunity to capitalize on possibilities in other areas of my life. While it was, undoubtedly, personally devastating, it absolutely was not an "F."

Marriages and relationships may not work out, for a variety of reasons, but they don't necessarily have to be categorized as an "F." Job opportunities may not materialize. Life may change course. The outcomes may not have been the original plan, but learning to reframe the type of lessons learned while pursuing those relationships, careers, and life goals is truly what matters.

Pivotal moments and complexities of life cannot simply be categorized into "P's" or "F's."

Scars

Since my shooting is long in my past, I can say with confidence that the experiences I have had, then and since, have had a profound impact on me and the person I have become. I have gained a great deal of wisdom. I certainly know I'm more passionate, more appreciative, more considerate, more empathetic, and more sympathetic. I'm far more emotional but I'm also more "all in"!

We all have battle scars. Some scars we wear on our bodies as physical realities, obvious to everyone, especially ourselves. Some scars we wear on our faces, often unbeknownst even to ourselves. We wear them in the unspoken facial expressions of pain, sadness, confusion, bewilderment, or denial. Some wounds are moral or emotional; some are psychological. Some injuries we verbalize, while others we communicate without ever saying a word. Some are "trophies" of things we have endured or conquered. Others we hide well, sharing them only with a select few. We each wear our battle scars differently, but regardless of how we got them, how we wear them, or how apparent they are to others, every single one of us has them.

A Hunter S. Thompson quote sums it up best. He says:

"Life should not be a journey to the grave with the intention of arriving safely in a pretty and well-preserved body, but rather to skid in broadside in a cloud of smoke, thoroughly used up, totally worn out, and loudly proclaiming "Wow! What a Ride!"

For years, I had that saying posted on my desk.

Naturally, I don't *treasure* having scars. I don't *want* the hidden ones like pain and PTSD, and I don't *want* the more obvious physical ones from my shooting and C-sections. Regardless, they represent monumental, life-changing moments, and all those scars, both visible and invisible, must be acknowledged and appreciated.

Scars truly do represent the stories of life.

Everyone Has a Story

One day while I was putting my prosthetic leg on, I noticed that my young son was watching me carefully. I also realized that I had sighed loudly while doing so. As I rose and put my weight on my leg, my son looked me in the eye and asked, "Does your leg make you sad?"

My initial reaction was to make light of it and brush it off. After all, as a mom, I want to model strength, independence, resilience, positivity. But this time, I chose to be direct. I looked at both of my kids and admitted, "Yeah, it makes me sad sometimes." I went on to explain that while I have a lot of good in my life, it doesn't take away from the fact that, quite simply, my leg does make me sad sometimes.

In that moment I was struck by several things. I appreciated that my son had matured to a level where he was able to get out of himself and his self-centred childish needs to empathize and be compassionate towards me. I was surprised by his intuition. And I was proud that I felt comfortable acknowledging my truth to both my children.

I have lost so many physical abilities and I feel as if my body has failed me. I think that's fair, and I give myself permission to grieve my losses. At times I feel disillusioned. I can be bitter. I might mourn. These feelings surface at unpredictable times. They remain for varying periods of time at varying levels of intensity.

I know I must acknowledge my emotions and allow myself time to be fully there in those emotions before I am able to refocus. Those phases continue to be critical because only then will I truly feel the happiness, the joy, that I now have confidence will eventually come. The dip into hopelessness and the subsequent rise into hopefulness allow me to experience happiness and satisfaction on an even deeper level, deeper *because* I have experienced such trauma. I now have the power to appreciate that pain is *not* insurmountable, and sadness *doesn't* last forever. I now trust that hope and optimism will inevitably take over. That knowledge, that conviction, drives me forward, one step at a time.

What I realized very soon after I lost my leg was that I am not all that unique. My story may be unique, but *everyone has a story*. Everyone has dealt with, or will deal with, loss, pain, grief. Those painful experiences are handed to us in a variety of ways—illness, death, disease, injury, trauma, divorce. What I have also realized is that despite the differences in story details, any of these experiences can elicit many of the same emotions. The pain I have experienced in my life is similar to the pain anyone else has experienced. Regardless of our individual journey and our differing circumstances, emotions are the equalizer. Anyone who has ever experienced loss can identify with the loss I have experienced. That person doesn't necessarily have to have been someone who experienced a gunshot or a leg amputation.

Loss is loss. Grief is grief. Pain is pain. It doesn't matter how it manifests itself or how we arrive there. I have learned that there is no range, no continuum of "worst" or "best." Our perception of another person's situation is based solely upon our personal experiences. We gauge others by using our own measuring stick, but those measuring sticks are not always accurate or truly reflective of reality.

What sets us apart as individuals is what we *do* with our stories, how we deal with loss and grief and pain. The most powerful skills we can possess are those that assist us in feeling the grief, allowing the loss to become absorbed, shifting our focus onto overcoming adversity, adapting to change, and becoming stronger, more self-aware and more resilient throughout the process.

Play-Doh

Having grown up in a small town in a family of quick-witted, athletic, and (arguably) good-looking brothers, naturally I often wondered where I fit into the world around me. I questioned who I was, what I wanted, where I was going.

I was a passionate figure skater, albeit not a very talented one. I am a sister, a daughter, a friend. I am a phys ed grad. I have a master's degree. I was a bartender (and a darned good one!). I was a skating coach. I was an aerobics instructor. I was a pretty fun substitute teacher. I was a Mountie.

I had worked so hard to establish myself, to find my place in the world, and when I thought I finally found it, I became "the one who got shot." My life, as I knew it, had shattered into a million pieces, and I felt that my only option was to rebuild what *used* to be. The only way forward, after years of finding myself, was to put every broken piece back together in the exact same way it had been before.

For so long, I tried desperately to do just that. I tried to go back in time, to be who I was, simply because I was unable to envision what next. Despite my best efforts, while I tried to become who I *had* been, the definitions of me continued to evolve. I became a wife for a while. I became a mom.

What I slowly realized is that while I am a complex combination of the descriptors above (and so many more), re-creating my pre-shooting existence was not only ridiculous, but an impossible goal. What was, was no longer, and what I had been seeking my whole life had always been fluid, often elusive, always changing anyway.

I realized that I had to quit looking backwards to find myself. I had to become a whole new original design. For me, that design became more of a mosaic, a variety of rigid, solid pieces representative of my past self. Those pieces were somewhat unchanged—my morals, my values, my background, my experiences. Other pieces, however, looked vastly different than anything I had envisioned. Instead of viewing myself as being one solid, unbreakable mass, I needed to reconstruct, and any leftover pieces had to be repositioned. I needed them, and they were crucial pieces of my being, but since they would never resemble their previous state, I needed to reinforce them. I needed to bond them back together in a viable way, as one does with Play-Doh. I recognized that while I craved the sturdiness, the perceived wholeness of my past, I also needed less rigidity, more malleability. If I could find a decent combination of all those things, I could retain the best of what had been, but allow for flexibility and adaptation going forward.

I now know there will be no identifiable result, no permanent, coveted, static shape. Individual combinations of genetics and life experiences can only lead to continuing complex transitions; that acceptance, that constant openness, will allow me to develop into more resilient and even stronger, versions of myself.

I Love You

When I was leaving for university once with a van full of friends waiting in the driveway, I hugged my dad goodbye. He was not a big hugger, and it was a bit awkward. In his ear, I whispered, "I love you." My dad stiffened, and I became aware that while I always knew he loved me and I knew he knew I loved him, I realized that we didn't *say* it.

As I considered that, I grew to believe that we had been relying on coexistence and physical proximity; those things gave us a built-in excuse to not bother with the actual words. They gave us permission to skip the statement. However, that moment in my driveway was powerful, and I promised myself that from that point on I would verbalize it more and more regularly.

In the last few years of my dad's life, I phoned him almost daily. Not one of those conversations ended without me telling him I loved him.

Leave notes. Write on Ziplocs in your kids' lunch kits. Send texts. Do the same for your partner. And don't forget your parents, your family members, your best friends.

Simply *knowing* there is love between two people is not enough. The actual words "I love you" matter.

Living My Dash

On three occasions, I have had the privilege of attending Campowerment, a program focused on empowering women and inspiring them to connect and find purpose. When I attended the first time, stressed by life and by work, alone and in search of direction and peace, I had no expectations. I just desperately needed a change of scenery and hoped for some motivation.

I found myself in a journaling session called "Live Your Dash," a poem by Linda Ellis. I had never heard it, but the poem explores the purpose of life by focusing on the dash separating two dates ... one's birth and one's death. The goal of the journaling exercise was to consider how we each were living our dashes.

Once the poem had been read, we were prompted to write down what we would *like* to be said about us at our funeral. It wasn't morbid in any way, simply something to contemplate while we analyzed our lives, who we were, how we were operating in the world.

We were then given some time to write quietly. But I was stuck. I sat there having no idea where to start, wondering what kinds of things might in fact be said about me in a eulogy. After several minutes of staring at my blank page, I slowly began to write. As I gained momentum, the words came to me faster and faster.

When it came time to share our thoughts with the group, I instantly welled up. By the time it was my turn to speak, I couldn't utter a word because I could barely breathe through my sobs. It was ugly crying—embarrassing, uncontrollable, and punctuated with gulps and snot.

What I realized that day was that I was *not* doing a good job of living my dash. For years, PTSD and trauma and fear had been monopolizing my actions, bullying me into focusing primarily on the second date in the poem: the death date.

That day at Camp, I acknowledged that that psychological preoccupation with the second date *must* stop if I wanted to ensure I leave a rich, meaningful legacy when that end date does in fact arrive. I also recognized that I had to change some things in my life in order to ensure I do just that.

I understood that my focus had to shift to living the small, seemingly insignificant, yet oh-so-critical dash.

Maintaining the Right

The RCMP motto is "Maintiens le droit". The simple translation is "uphold the law" or "maintain the right," and there is irony that I lost my right leg while trying desperately to do exactly that.

I do believe that my situation was, in many ways, groundbreaking for the RCMP, and I recognize that those early experiences were further complicated by the lack of sophisticated technology of the day. However, despite the personal sacrifice, I hold onto the conviction that my shooting and my subsequent return to work have been fundamental in promoting some degree of positive organizational change. My journey and the timing of the issues I faced highlighted some gaps within the organization, and I am confident that my responses to those issues over the years have been beneficial for the membership at large.

Granted, tens of thousands of members have had far lengthier careers than I, but few (fortunately) will say that they survived being shot. That experience alone has afforded me a unique experience, one that warrants being shared. But the "being shot in 1998" part is only a starting point. The challenges and obstacles I faced lasted the duration of my career and will continue for the rest of my life. That adversity shaped my perspective, and after all, perspective really is one's reality.

When I signed my retirement papers and left the organization in January 2020, it was a highly emotional time. But my shooting had resulted in so many physical, emotional, and professional challenges over more than two decades, and the cumulative impact was a heavy load to carry. I was torn about leaving the Force, although I knew deep down it was time. I needed to spend more time focusing on my health—for me and for my family.

I had finally realized the soundness behind one airline safety protocol; I needed to put my own oxygen mask on before helping others. It was time for change. For self-preservation, I chose to put on my own mask.

10-35

Since March 11, 1996, I always felt, on some level, as if I were "on duty." Being an RCMP officer defined me in many ways and despite the pride I had in wearing my uniform, I also grew to resent it on occasion. I wanted to kick back, relax, and not feel like my actions were being judged and scrutinized. I wanted to be free of the responsibility, real or perceived, that I felt as an RCMP officer.

In the early years, I stifled and lost parts of myself because I accepted that anonymity was not part of my existence. It was simply a luxury reserved for other people. I became hyper-aware of feeling I was always being watched, whether at work or not. Often it was, as they say, like living under a microscope.

As time wore on and I relocated to larger communities, what I did for a living was not nearly as much of a factor in how I carried on with my daily routines. The awareness was lessened because I was living in more populated areas, and I didn't occupy uniformed positions or drive RCMP-marked police cars. Still, I had that nagging notion that everyone recognized me, and as a result, they had higher expectations of me. After all, I had once been suddenly and unexpectedly thrust into the public eye, and the feeling that it could happen again at any time, although highly unlikely, made me anxious and wary.

Now I contemplate my years of serving the public, of wearing my red serge with tremendous pride. I greatly appreciate the numerous once-in-a-lifetime experiences my career offered. I will continue to cherish the countless outstanding people I have had the good fortune of welcoming into my life because of being a Mountie. I will forever become emotional at the impressive sight of a sea of RCMP members in red serge, marching en masse. But

I also mourn the sacrifices I have made, and I honour the ones that others like me have made, to help our country to be a better and safer place.

I look around at all I have in my life now and I celebrate the ups, try not to get too disappointed in the downs. I have learned to accept the ebbs and flows, the trials, the tribulations, the challenges, with a little less drama and a smidge more patience. Ultimately, I have learned to better appreciate the successes and the triumphs.

I have hope. I believe in the power of perseverance. I understand who I was, who I used to be. I accept what I've lost, but I try my damnedest to focus on what I have gained. I am resilient and I am fortunate to have a fulfilling life full of love.

I have also accepted that "getting there" is *not* the ultimate goal because "there" is not a tangible place. Instead, I am learning to welcome the evolution, the growth, the transformation experienced by simply forging ahead. Quite literally, it means taking one step at a time.

For me, words of the ancient Chinese philosopher/writer Lao Tsu couldn't ring truer:

"A journey of a thousand miles begins with a single step."

I am officially, and permanently ... **10-35** (radio code for **"Off Duty"**).

[END]